CHASING AMERICA
Of Lollipops, Night Clubs and Ferocious Dogs.

Deepak Singh

SUPERNOVA
PUBLISHERS

First published in 2011
by
Supernova Publishers & Distributors Pvt Ltd
12, ARD Complex
R.K. Puram, Sector 13
New Delhi 110066
www.supernovapublishers.com
supernova.publishers@gmail.com

Copyright © Deepak Singh 2011
Printed and bound in India by Replika Press Pvt. Ltd.

ISBN 978-81-89930-49-3

Deepak Singh asserts the moral right
to be identified as the author of this work

For
Anushka

Contents

~

Acknowledgements

~

I would especially like to thank my wife who said it was okay for me to write this book. She showed a lot of patience when I left her and my daughter alone for several hours during the day for many months to complete this project. Without her support, this book would have remained confined to a folder on my computer.

Art Collier is another person who has made this book possible. He read every chapter several times, and guided me and provided me direction. Thank you, Art!

I want to thank Janis Jaquith, Sean Tubbs, Lynn Uhl, and Phil McEldowney for their words of encouragement. Special thanks to Ram Advani and Udayan Singh for putting their faith in me as a first-time writer.

I am grateful to people at the Writer House in Charlottesville, especially Rachel Unkefer, Elizabeth McCullough, and Christy. They answered my questions and helped me when I needed advice, a book to read, or a place to write.

I would also like to say thanks to the staff at the Greenberry's on Barracks road in Charlottesville. They provided me with a friendly atmosphere and a comfortable place to write.

Finally, I would like to thank the people in rural Pennsylvania, who opened their homes and their lives to someone who came to them both as a stranger and as family.

Leaving India

~

The flight to Washington DC was booked for September 10th, 2003—my first intercontinental journey. I was leaving my parents' home, for the first time, to start a new life in a new country with my wife, Holly, whom I had met and married in my hometown, Lucknow. My parents were worried about me. Would my wife treat me well? Would my in-laws like me? Would I be able to find a job? And what if the weather didn't suit me? I assured them—not sure myself—that I would be fine.

A lot of my relatives, including my parents, came to see me off at the train station, but only my brother came all the way to New Delhi. It was easier to meet everyone in Lucknow and exchange hugs, take innumerable hints from my mother about eating well, and instructions from my dad about not consuming alcohol in America.

I spent my last day in India meeting all my friends in New Delhi and doing last minute shopping. My old friend

Sid—a native of Delhi—made sure I ate some of the local food before I left. He took me to the old part of the city and we spent a few hours walking around the Red Fort and *Chandni Chowk* market and sampled sweets from our favorite *mithai* shop. We both knew it was going to be a few years before we could do this again.

While I was sad that I was going away from my family and friends, I was eager to see my wife. After running around Delhi for many hours I came back to my friend's place to clean up and get ready to go to the airport.

I took a shower and repacked my suitcases for the ninth time and made sure I had everything—passport, visa, tickets, money—accessible for immediate use while boarding the plane. I had been asking people who had travelled abroad earlier to give me a rundown of the procedure involved in checking yourself into the flight.

Realizing how involved the process was, I made a list of things to do—don't lock your suitcases for baggage check-in, show the right ticket to get the boarding pass, don't bring food items, bring my passport—in a notebook and flipped through the pages several times, to make sure I had everything under control.

Since I am a nervous and a generally confused traveler, I often show up at the wrong platform for the wrong train for the wrong destination at the wrong time. Once, when my wife was visiting me in India, we went on a vacation to Manali, a small city in the mountains of north India. I booked our tickets a month before, and checked several times to make sure all the details were correct on the railway ticket. Everything looked good and we showed up at the train station an hour before the departure.

The train arrived and we got on to our compartment, found our seats and quickly shoved our luggage under them and plunked ourselves down on it, taking a deep breath, looking in each other's eyes with a smile that said, "We are all set." When the train shuffled off, a middle-aged man with a giant watermelon-sized belly, wearing a loose-fitting white shirt and pajamas came and sat down next to me—allowing his thigh to touch mine—and started wiping his face with a towel. Adjusting my legs, I asked him, "Which is your seat?" He replied with a smile, "The one you are sitting on."

"This is my seat," I said, "Check your ticket, you must be wrong." He replied, "I have been travelling in this seat for the last eight hours."

I showed him our ticket and pointed at the train number, destination, date, and the day. He checked everything twice on our ticket and pointed out something that we had missed even after checking several times. We were travelling on the right train, on the right date, on the right day, but the wrong month—we had the tickets for the next month. Now we were on a moving train with the wrong ticket and no seats. Since I had never been on a train without a ticket, I started panicking and wanted to get off the train at the next station, but my wife calmed me down and advised that I should talk to the ticket examiner. She also suggested that I leave our bags with her while I sorted out the matter. I later realized that it was a very smart move by her because had she been with me while negotiating with the ticket examiner, I would have had to pay a much higher 'fine' in order to find us seats. Firstly, the guy would have raised his eyebrows at me after seeing that I was with a white woman; he would have judged me—thinking that I must be after her money or something even worse—looking at me from head to toe, and if I could shut him up by proving that she was my wife, he would have charged me more money anyway. I approached the man in black coat and white trousers who was counting money, wetting his thumb after flipping every rupee. I said, "Sir, I have a problem." He ignored me and continued counting, pressing his thumb on his *paan*-stained red tongue. I waited for a few minutes and when he stopped, I explained him the whole situation. He looked at me and shifted the chewed lump of tobacco and betel leaf in his mouth from one side to the other and said, "Let me see your ticket." When I presented the tickets to him, he pointed his steel flashlight at it and shifted his spectacled eyes between the tickets and my face, as if he was trying to decide how much money he could get out of me. After a pause of a few seconds he said, "One thousand rupees plus the cost of the ticket." I must have looked pitiful as I was expecting him to ask for much more. We managed to get ourselves new tickets.

As a result of gaffes in my previous travel adventures, I was extra cautious and extremely nervous. A seventeen-hour international fight was a big deal. I arrived at the airport in New Delhi five hours before the plane was set to depart. It was eleven at night and people with duffle bags, handbags, and suitcases piled on push-carts were waiting to get inside the airport through the gates designated for their airlines. Some of the western travelers looked dirty, shabbily dressed and tired as if they had had enough of India's heat, dust and pollution and couldn't wait to get on the plane. Indian passengers also looked anxious but they seemed to have their best clothes on. Like me, many of them had brought at least five people who had come to see them off.

I took a deep breath and realized that I had arrived at a place which was the point of no return. I was going to take off in a few hours and did not know when I would return. I got into a line leading to a gate for my airline. I tried to talk to some of the fellow passengers in line and asked where they were going. None of them seemed to be on my flight. My turn came to get inside the airport.

"You are way too early, come back after two hours." The gatekeeper at the gate said to me after looking at my ticket.

I replied, "Why can't I go inside the airport? I have a ticket and a valid visa."

"You are allowed inside the airport only three hours before the flight departs. You are here five hours before."

I found out that due to security concerns, passengers were not allowed to enter the airport more than three hours before the flight. After the gatekeeper told me to wait, I moved my luggage cart around and wheeled it across the street and went inside a waiting room. The place was filled with backpackers lying on blue colored chairs with their heads resting on their backpacks, marked with patches of sweat. I parked my cart near an empty seat. A scruffy white boy was sitting next to me; he was scribbling something on a palm-sized notebook. I looked at him and he gave me a tight-lipped smile and continued writing. I asked him where he was going. "London," he said, "my flight's no' leaving until tomorrow morning, though." I asked him why he'd come to the airport eighteen hours early. He replied, "It's much cheape' than a ho-el room, mate, in-i'!"

When I told him that I was travelling to America for the first time, he said, "They go' some fast cars there... they go like shi' off the shovel."

"So I hear."

"Can you drive, mate?"

"Actually, I can't."

"You'll be alrigh'. As long as you can ge' in the car and shu' the do', you will be fine...they are all gearless... easy peasy, mate!"

After talking to him for a while, we started to move towards the gate again. At this point, everybody who had come to see me off had already left, except my friend Sid. I was getting anxious thinking of going through security, baggage claim, immigration and customs, etc. I just wanted to get on the plane. I could not wait for the full two hours and showed up at the gate about thirty minutes before the gatekeeper told me to come.

"I told you to come back in two hours." He said.

I was more determined this time and looked into his eyes and said, "Look, my mistake is that I am here early, not late. This is the first time I am travelling abroad and

I want to give myself enough time to go through all the formalities."

He took pity on me and let me inside the airport. Now, I had to figure out my next step. I went to check my baggage in. I had two suitcases that needed to be checked in. One was red and the other green.

They had to go through the security check. I gave both of them to the airport staff. The red suitcase made it through the X-ray machine. Someone pulled it out the other end and put a tag on the handle. It seemed like everything was going to be okay and I started to feel a little relaxed. But then a police officer shouted as my next suitcase went through the X-ray machine, "Hold on to that green suitcase." He asked me, "What do you have in it?" Before I could answer his question he rudely asked me to open it. I hesitated because there were a few things in it that I would have rather shown in private than in front of fifty people under bright lights.

I looked at the officer and he stared back at me and looked at the suitcase, asking me with his eyes to hurry up. As soon as I opened it, he ruffled my carefully packed, neatly arranged suitcase. My mother and I had spent hours arranging and re-arranging it so that everything fit well. We had packed some sweets, pickles, medicine, undergarments, that sort of thing. I was nervous and very sad, but what really made me embarrassed was what that police officer pulled out of the suitcase. It was a pressure cooker.

My wife wanted me to bring it with me because she enjoyed cooking Indian food and she had learned to cook from my mother who used a pressure cooker for a lot of dishes. But before she could have it, this guy hoisted our brand new, shiny, stainless steel pressure cooker—like a trophy—acting as if he had won it by catching me. The X-Ray machine got confused by its shape and sent strange signals. After causing a bit of a commotion, he let me repack my suitcase, including the pressure cooker.

That incident shook my confidence as I moved forward to go through the next ordeal. After checking in the luggage, I had to get the boarding pass. The lady at the check-in counter asked to see my visa for America and the ticket. She tore off a part of the ticket and gave it to me and said, "Happy journey!"

I asked her in a state of total disbelief, "Is that all?"

She smiled and said, "Next, please!"

I moved forward to the next hurdle which was the immigration check. I had to show my passport and visa one more time. The police officer asked me before he examined my passport, "What's your father's name?", and looked in the passport to confirm my answer. He looked at the picture in the passport and looked at my face. His forehead wrinkled as he looked at me one more time, holding the passport up in the air. His eyes moved rapidly between an open page in the passport and my face.

I sensed some trouble. I thought that was the end of my race. There was no way he was going to let me get on the plane without putting me through some serious interrogation. He took me by surprise when he returned my passport, and said, "You look good without a moustache. Don't grow it back."

I had sported a moustache around the time I had gotten my passport photos taken, but had shaved it off just before my wedding.

After clearing immigration, I went through customs without any trouble. The security officers ran their metal detectors over my body and wished me a safe trip. As I walked out of the rectangular metal detector gate, I felt like a mouse who had escaped through a hole after being chased by a cat. Through with all the formalities, and feeling relaxed, I wandered around the airport, called my parents, and browsed through the duty free shops before it was time to board the plane.

Soon, they announced my flight and asked people to start boarding. I got into the line behind a guy draped in saffron robe, head to toe. He was going to be a *pujari*, a priest in some Hindu temple in Washington, DC. The person in front of me was a visiting professor of Mathematics at a university.

My turn came and I walked on to the plane. Two happy looking air hostesses welcomed me, "Welcome aboard!" and pointed me in the direction of my seat, after looking at the boarding pass. As I walked in, I saw some people were trying to jostle suitcases twice the size of the storage space above the seats and others who had already taken up more storage space than they were allowed, were getting cozy in their seats, covering themselves with the blankets and putting on headphones supplied by the airline.

I got to my seat to find that there was an elderly Indian couple sitting there. Before I said anything to them, the man requested me to sit in his seat. I took their seat and put my stuff under the seat in front. After making myself comfortable, I got up and walked inside the plane, the cabin of which was wider than any of my family's homes. After a few minutes, everyone settled down and the plane took off. As the aircraft gained height the twinkling lights of Delhi got further and further away in the oval shaped window. I thought of my parents and friends whom I was leaving behind and felt sad. The combination of fatigue and emotions caused me to fall asleep soon. I must have been very tired to sleep through the whole flight. I woke up only when they announced that we were about to land in Vienna, Austria.

As soon as I stepped out of the plane in Vienna airport, I was questioned by two men wearing a black dress that had *Polizie* written across it. They asked to see my passport and questioned me about my next destination after Vienna. They gave back my passport after looking at it for thirty seconds and wished me happy journey. I walked around the Vienna airport, which looked much different than the airport in Delhi. Within seven hours and five thousand miles, a lot—people, language, signs, food—had changed. All the cafes, souvenir shops and payphones accepted only Euros. The signs were in a German and people were mostly white.

I realized I did not prepare for this part—a six-hour layover—of my journey. Since I did not have any Euros or any kind of international credit cards, I spent six hours without eating. I wanted to call my parents, but the pay phone only took Euro coins. After walking around and browsing through gift shops for a few hours, it was time to get on the plane again.

This time I managed to sit in my own seat, and now the person next to me was a young Indian Sikh. After a few minutes, I found out that he could not speak English or Hindi. He understood what I said in Hindi, but replied back in Punjabi, and I barely understood what he said, but between a few words in both the languages, and some gesticulation, we bonded.

Like me, he was traveling to the States for the first time. He told me he was going to be a car mechanic in his uncle's shop in Atlanta. He seemed to be a nice guy, but the thing that bothered me about him was that he poked his elbow into my ribs every time an air hostess passed by. He did that to make me ask the air hostess to give him more wine. After serving wine several times to this guy—who was determined to finish every single bottle available in the aircraft—the air hostesses stopped coming through our aisle. I felt like telling the air hostess to give him a strong dose of rum to make him fall asleep and stop bothering me and them.

After a few hours of listening to music, watching a movie, and sleeping, I heard the pilot declare that we were getting ready to descend in the American capital. It was 3:30 in the afternoon and the temperature in Washington, DC, was seventy-two degrees Fahrenheit. I noticed the houses—which appeared like tiny dots neatly marked in rows—when the plane flew over a residential area. As the plane circled around the airport to land, I could see vehicles on wide streets moving in an orderly fashion. I was ecstatic to think that my wife could be driving one of those cars to come to get me from the airport.

The plane landed safely and it taxied to a terminal at the Dulles airport. As we got off, we were directed to go in different directions, according to the kind of visa we had. US citizens went in one direction, permanent residents in the other direction, and so forth. My turn came and the officer gestured me to come up to him.

I showed him my passport and the visa. He looked at it and keyed some numbers into his computer. He then asked me to put my finger on a machine to get my finger print.

"Are you sure you were born in India and not Pakistan?" he asked me with a stern looking face.

"Yes, I am," I answered, looking at him, puzzled.

"What is the purpose of your visit?"

"To be with my wife…"

"Where did you meet her?"

"Lucknow, India."

"Where did you get married?"

"India."

"How long are you going to stay in the US?"

"A few years…"

After flipping through my passport for the fifteenth time, "…alright, you are good to go," he said, not being able to find a reason to interrogate me further.

I walked away from him wondering what in my passport – issued in India – suggested that I was born in Pakistan. I was born in Lucknow, which is at least five hundred miles from the Pakistani border. Puzzled about why he asked such a question, I looked at my watch to adjust the time and I noticed the date—10th September—a day before the 9/11 anniversary. Maybe that explained the police officer's behavior towards me.

I took a deep breath, thankful that the hell was over and that I had finally arrived in the United States of America—the land of the free, the promised land.

Just Arrived

~

I was happy to see my suitcases slowly tumbling towards me on the airport carousel; they looked quite beat up, as if they had been thrown around a lot—the joints seemed loose and the covers, scratched. While I grabbed one of them, the other moved away on the fast-moving strip, making me run after it. I loaded my luggage on an abandoned cart and started pushing it towards a gate that said, "Exit." Airport authorities were dressed in dark blue uniforms and carried walkie-talkies in their hands, announcing flight numbers. "United 2103, Gate 14, United 2147, Gate 7." It was strange to be surrounded by people who spoke English in an American accent. I had watched American movies in India, but the people at the airport sounded different to me.

I noticed a female airport official was trying to talk to an African woman who was wearing a traditional, bright-colored, loose dress which covered her from head to toe.

She seemed to have just arrived and spoke no English. I overheard the airport worker ask, "Is someone coming to pick you up, Ma'am?" The African woman smiled—revealing her white teeth—in response to the question. She asked her again and got another big grin in return. I paused for a moment to see what was going on but the official gave me a look that meant, "It's not your business." I looked away and started trudging forward.

I came into the visitors' area of the airport to find Holly—she was coming to pick me up. Expecting her to be waiting for me, I looked around for a while, but didn't see her. After waiting for a few minutes I thought of giving her a call to find out where she was. I saw a payphone near a cafeteria, but I didn't have any American coins. This was a good opportunity for me to use my first hundred dollar bill that I had gotten from the State Bank of India in Lucknow. Excited about making my first purchase in America, I looked for something to drink in the cafeteria window. Among a dozen different items, I could only recognize one—diet Coke. It was $1.29. I picked it up eagerly and took out the biggest bill to pay for it. "Don't you have anything smaller?" said the cashier. Since he looked Indian, I asked "Where are you from, sir?" "New Delhi," he said, without making eye contact with me. I told him I had just arrived and had no other way of paying. He took my money irritably and gave the change back. It was funny that after traveling for ten thousand miles my first encounter in America was with an Indian.

As I started using the phone, a white-haired, overweight airport official walked by and said, "You can't make no calls from that phone." I looked at him and continued dialing the number. The phone didn't seem to connect the line. I wasn't ready to believe this. I was in America and everything was supposed to work here. In the meantime, the same guy walked back and said, "I told you, you can't make no calls from that phone. It don't work!" I was confused because he seemed to be contradicting himself. First, he used two negatives in the sentence which meant, "Yes, you can make phone calls," and then he said, "It don't work."

I gave up and asked a fellow traveler if he would let me call my wife on his cell phone. He did, and I found out that she was on her way to the airport. Since I had some time to kill, I sat down on a chair near the cafeteria. Minutes later, a young man with a kid came and sat down next to me; he had a bunch of balloons—that said 'Welcome Back'—tied to his baby's wrist. He gave me a smile and I noticed that he was trying to read the address on the cover of my suitcase, written in large letters. He looked at me and smiled again. I could tell he wanted to talk so I said, "I just arrived…it's my first day." "Oh yeah," he exclaimed, "You mean first day in DC?"

"Actually, it's my first day in America."

"Wow, congratulations, welcome to America…my name is Chris by the way."

"Thanks, I am Deepak."

"I see you are from India."

"Yes, I am."

"Are you waiting for someone to pick you up?"

When I said my wife was coming from Charlottesville, Virginia, he told me he was waiting for his wife to return from Israel. Waiting for our wives to arrive, we chatted about various things—learning to drive in the US, what kind of work I might be interested in, how I met Holly, and whether I had met her family yet. After an hour or so, I started wondering where Holly was. Chris said, "She might be stuck on the Beltway."

I didn't know what the Beltway was and just when I was going to ask, my wife showed up in jeans and a t-shirt. I couldn't recognize her at first, since I had always seen her wearing *salwar kameez*, Indian tunics and trousers in India. I asked, "Were you stuck on the Beltway?" She said, "Yes, but how do you know about the Beltway?" I told her that the person sitting next to me in the waiting area mentioned it to me. I later learned that it is an interstate highway that circles Washington, D.C. and its inner suburbs. I said goodbye to Chris and thanked him for the company. I gathered my stuff and got ready to leave.

When I came out of the Dulles airport in Washington, DC, I realized that I hadn't inhaled fresh air in the last twenty-four hours—I had spent seventeen hours inside the plane, and seven hours inside the airport in Vienna. American air felt crisp and fresh, I took a deep breath and filled my lungs with it. At four in the afternoon the sun was not at its strongest; there was a nip in the air. Twenty-four hours ago, at eleven o'clock at night, outside Indira Gandhi International airport in New Delhi, the air had felt heavy with fumes, and the climate, muggy.

Holly had driven her Oldsmobile sedan—a very large, four-door American car—from Charlottesville. As we pushed the luggage cart out of the airport, I saw a sea of cars parked in front of us—Toyotas, Hondas, Fords, BMWs, Mercedes, Chevrolets, and many more. After we walked through the maze of vehicles for a while, she asked me to find her car among the thousand other vehicles in the parking lot. She had shown me some pictures of her car on the internet, but that was not enough for me to tell which one was hers.

She popped the trunk of the car open with her remote control to give me a clue. I walked to the car and was amazed to see the massive trunk, which swallowed my two suitcases and a handbag, and still had room for a human being to fit in it. The interior of the car was big enough to seat at least eight people. The doors of the car were at least eight inches thick and there was twice as much leg room as I had on the plane. Wondering why anyone would need such a huge car, especially when he or she was the only person using it, I questioned my wife about the size of the vehicle. "My grandparents want us to be safe," she explained.

After we got settled in the car, she handed me a sheet of paper which said, 'MapQuest Directions' at the top. "I need your help with directions to get out of here," she said. I could not understand what "Take the ramp toward I-495/Washington/VA-28/US-50/VA-7/Sterling/Centreville" meant. I asked, "How is this supposed to help you get out of here?" She replied, "Just read it to me," as she pulled on to a four-lane road. I started to get the feeling that my wife was acting differently than she did in India. She sounded authoritative. In India, I drove her everywhere on the back of my scooter and made most of the day-to-day decisions. This was the first time I was the passenger and she was sitting in the driver's seat.

I kept reading whatever was there on the sheet, without making any sense of the combination of numbers and letters like I-495, VA-7, US-50, etc. Somehow, those things made sense to her. Every time she had to change lanes she would turn back—as if she wanted to jump into the back seat—to see whether the road was clear. It was amazing. I hadn't seen anyone looking back while they drove.

As we went along, we were often surrounded on both sides by huge trucks with signs that said WAL-MART, FED EX and MCDONALDS, etc. And, it would be like that for quite a distance as the trucks were—at least they seemed like—a mile long. It was like driving between two gigantic billboards with American advertisements.

It reminded me of a scene from some Hollywood movie where a newcomer in New York is gaping at advertisements covering the whole length of a building. Between reading directions from the sheet to my wife and obeying her other orders—pass me the water, change the CD—I watched us go under several flyovers that seemed like curled up spaghetti in the sky. Somewhere along the way I fell asleep and started dreaming about being in America and people yelling at me in very obscene language. I was shortly woken up to find myself at a gas station that was painted red and had *Sheetz* written all over it. Our car was parked next to a red convertible and my wife was filling up the tank, holding the nozzle in her hands.

I shook my head to regain my alertness. The red car parked next to us had loud and strange music playing, and the lyrics sounded something like this: ----- motherf*$k#r ----- f&c* you ----- motherf*$k#r ----- f&c* you ----- f&c* you ----- motherf*$k#r

There was a guy sitting in the passenger's side of the car and another one filling up the tank. The person inside the car was throwing his both hands up in the air as if he was giving someone a massage; he had his head tilted at a forty-five degree angle, and moved it to the music's deep bass—lowering it and then raising, lowering it and then raising it—in a rhythmic fashion. As the song progressed it picked up speed, and so did the head and hand motions of the person; he poked his hands in the air and bobbled his head with more intensity, as if he and the music were one. He also lip-synced the song, biting his lower lip every two seconds, making an angry face.

My half-awake mind found the song disturbing. Holly filled the gas tank and pushed some buttons on the machine to get a receipt. She asked me if I wanted to use the restroom inside the store. I said yes and followed her.

Inside, we were greeted by a happy-looking old white woman who was wearing a blue shirt with lots of round clip-on buttons that said, "Employee of the month," "Customer first," and "Sheetz." The store appeared to be a very lively place, and it had nice music playing everywhere.

It did not have the same kind of lyrics as the red car outside. I picked up a bottle of water, and went to one of the cashiers to pay. The lady smiled at me and asked, "How ya doin' today?" I said, "I am doing fine." I thought it was really nice of her to ask even though I didn't know her, but wondered why she added "today" at the end of her sentence—it was the first time I had seen her. I said, "I have just arrived from India, though." She cocked one eyebrow and said, "Long way away from home, arentcha?" I said, "Indeed." As I walked out of the line, I heard her say, "How ya doin' today?" to the next person, and before I left the store she asked that question of several more people. I wondered why she didn't care to ask people if they had been well the day before or a week before.

I kept awake for the rest of the journey. The excitement of being in America was getting muddled up with the anxiety about sharing a house with strangers in Charlottesville. My wife had told me about this before, but the idea of living with strangers in America started to sink in only when I saw the sign, "CHARLOTTESVILLE 6."

Housemates

~

Lights came on to illuminate the driveway when we parked our car in front of a red-brick house. I asked Holly whether someone had turned the lights on. "No, they're automatic," she said. I got out of the car and saw a sign, "615" mounted above the main entrance of the house. It was a number that I had been using, for more than a year, as an address to send letters to Holly from India. It was surreal that I was standing in front of it and that I was going to live in it. The house had a small grassy area in front. A couple of small steps led to the front door. I was expecting other housemates to be there, but didn't see anyone. Holly gave me a quick tour of the place. The house had three levels—basement, first floor, and second floor. The first floor—it would be ground floor in India—of the house had a staircase in the middle that worked as a divider between the study and the living room; the wooden floors and the staircase squeaked as we walked.

An old, but comfortable-looking sofa, a dining table with a slightly warped top, six chairs, several shelves—so tightly packed with books that I had to use both hands to get one out—and a television set filled the living room. One of the shelves had an assortment of bottles of alcohol, and there were at least twenty of them. The other half of the first floor was used as a study and a kitchen. There were books and papers everywhere in the study area—huge piles stacked up against the walls, on the desk, on the floor. There was a path to walk through them. Some of the area that was not covered with books and papers had cables of different colors running across the room. Holly showed me the kitchen and said that it was a common place to cook; any of the house members could cook there, provided they used their own groceries. She mentioned that all members of the house paid rent in equal parts and were supposed to share the housework.

The second floor of the house had three bedrooms, two small-sized and one large. My wife had the biggest room. After looking around I noticed there were no light bulbs attached to the walls or ceiling; the entire area was illuminated by lamps of different sizes, placed randomly around the house. I brought my luggage into our room and put my passport, wallet, and other important things into a drawer that Holly had emptied for me. The walls in her room had decorations and wall hangings that I had sent her or she had brought back from India. While I was still taking in everything, Holly brought me a cordless phone and asked me to call my parents and tell them I had arrived in Charlottesville. She told me she had bought twenty dollars' worth of minutes for me to call home. I had an awful time getting connected; I had to dial a toll-free number, a sixteen-digit pin number, country code, city code and then my home phone number, and I had to do all of that several times because I was too tired to get it right in one attempt. Finally, I heard my mother's voice at the other end. I had never talked to my mother from so far away. When I told her that I had just arrived in Charlottesville, she got quiet for a minute and then said, "Did you have your breakfast?" I said it was dinner time in America and asked her what time it was in India. She said, "We are getting ready to have breakfast." I could tell my mother was trying her best not to cry, and so was I. After talking to her for a few minutes, I promised to call her the next day and ended the conversation. Seeing tears welling up in my eyes, Holly held my hand and gave me a hug. I was torn between emotions—the sadness of being away from my parents and the excitement of being united with Holly. It had been more than fifty hours since I had left Lucknow. I couldn't keep myself awake and soon fell asleep.

The next morning, I woke up with the sun shining in my face and people talking on the street. In India, I was used to waking up to different kinds of noises, a vegetable vendor hawking down the street, a scrap dealer shouting his lungs out, or a beggar wailing. At first, the people talking outside the house in Charlottesville sounded like one of those noises in India, but when I became fully awake, I realized they were talking in English and that I was in America. It was 9 am, and I could hear Holly's voice downstairs. I must have been deep asleep since I didn't hear her getting out of bed. While I was still gathering my thoughts, Holly called me downstairs for breakfast.

I went down and saw Keith and Liz, the other members of the house, sitting at the dining table. We shook hands and introduced ourselves. Keith was a broad-shouldered, tall man with brawny arms. He had a big neck with a pair of muscles that rose up from his black shirt. His long brown curls hid his jaws every time he leaned forward to grab a bite from his sandwich. He seemed friendly.

Liz was a tallish woman who had light brown hair and carried a few extra pounds. Her style of talking took some getting used to. She pronounced her vowels with a matching facial expressions and usually ended her sentences with a rising intonation as if she meant it to be a question. She used wild metaphors and everything she said sounded enigmatic. But, everything she said was intelligent. She seemed to be friendly and reserved at the same time. She answered most of my questions in Yeps and Nopes—not allowing me to take the conversation further. After a brief conversation with the two of them, I looked down and saw toasted round bread with a hole in the middle and a glass of cranberry juice in front of me. I bit the crisp exterior and enjoyed the chewy part in the middle of it—it was my first bagel. I sat there and ate breakfast while Holly, Liz, and Keith watched the weather forecast on television and talked about how warm it had been recently. It reminded me of the last breakfast in India at my parents' home where my mother had cooked gloriously greasy *parathas,* fried flat bread, and served them hot, straight from the pan to my plate. Since I tend to overeat she generally scolds me if I eat more than I should, but that day—since I was leaving for the United States the next day—she let me eat more than usual. She knew I would miss her food in America.

On my second day in Charlottesville, my wife invited some of her friends—Dwight, Angela, and Ann—to have dinner at our place and meet me. The couple, Dwight and Angela, had cooked and brought burgers with them. They wanted me to try some American food. Dwight was a short-haired white man, more than six feet tall, and his broad chest and fat muscular neck made him look like a soccer player. He also spoke like a soccer player—loud and abusive; he didn't speak a sentence without a swear word in it. He served me two big greasy burgers. When I asked him about what kind of burgers they were, he said, "Ham!" It immediately brought to mind pigs rolling in sewage water. I told him that I had never eaten pork and imagining pigs in India aroused a feeling of disgust in me. He responded, "This is beef!" I told him I didn't eat beef either and that cows are sacred in India. He was quick to say, "American cows aren't scared. Eat it!" My jet-lagged mind was still recovering from the onslaught of strange experiences in the big land and Dwight wasn't helping me by using harsh language.

I started picking at the burger, reluctantly, while everyone else stuffed their mouths with big chunks. After asking me about my journey from India, and whether I was enjoying my time in Charlottesville, Dwight's girlfriend started complaining that she couldn't find the right bra for herself. I was surprised at the sudden change of topic and totally taken aback to hear a woman talk about her bra in front of other people and especially in front of me, a man she had never met. I took a quick swig from a glass filled with water and pushed a piece of meat that I had been struggling with down my throat. I had barely removed the glass from my lips when I heard Dwight say, "It's because you change sizes too often." I had never heard a man talk about his significant other's breasts. I remember my mother often left my father and me alone for a few minutes when we went shopping for clothes. As a child, I was always curious and asked her about what she bought when she returned with a plastic bag. She would try to avoid my question but when I nagged her she'd respond, "Ladies' products!" Although she doesn't speak fluent English, she would use those two English words in a way that made me shut up and not ask any more questions. I grew up and learned that there are certain things about women you shouldn't ask and joke about. It was shocking to hear Dwight mock his lady's cup size in public.

I ignored Dwight and Angela's conversation and tried to talk to Ann. When I asked her what she did for a living, her big round eyes sparkled as if she had been waiting for me to ask that question. She explained, with a big grin on her face, that she taught and counseled people about how to practice safe sex. She said, "Actually, I just got off work." She opened a box full of oddly shaped objects and asked, "Would you like me to show you what I do?" Before I could say yes, she had two of those items in her hand. I had never seen or heard about any of those things before and didn't know what they were supposed to do. Ann told me that each of them had names—Dream Maker Lunar Rabbit, Lovemoiselle Cecile, Turbo Accelerator and Safe Silicone. Still confused, I looked at her as if she was speaking a language that I didn't understand. It began to make sense when Ann started demonstrating. I almost died from embarrassment, but Ann's hands weren't shy of pointing at her body parts to explain how the toys worked.

Ann reminded me of my Biology teacher in India. When we reached the part of our textbook about the reproductive system, she made us read the whole chapter in class, in front of her, making sure each student read at least one paragraph out loud. All of us desperately hoped we wouldn't get the paragraph that described human genitalia. One of my friends did have to read that dreaded part and we teased him the whole year about how embarrassed he was and how much fun we had watching his face turn red. If that friend of mine had seen Ann demonstrating those toys to me, I am sure he would have taken his revenge and given me a hard time about how awkward I felt.

I spent the whole evening listening to Dwight's monologue—adorned with swear words—about how he made the best burgers, his girlfriend's frustrations about not being able to find good undergarments, and learning about the Turbo Accelerator and Safe Silicone.

My head began to ache from the information overload. The second day in America had already started to feel like a long time. I was beginning to find the place and the people foreign, and myself, dislocated. I couldn't get anything familiar. The thing that was most unsettling was that my wife—whom I had only seen and known in India—was also acting different in the company of her friends. It seemed to me that it didn't bother her that her friends used obscene language. She seemed to be a different person.

I thought things would change once I started working. Since my work permit was going to take at least three months to arrive, I tried to keep myself entertained by listening to Hindi music that I had brought from India and by reading books that Holly brought from the university library. Often when Holly was in her class or meeting her professor, I stayed on the second floor, confined to our room. But, sometimes after listening to eighty three songs and reading hundreds of pages from a book, I felt like doing something else.

One day when I had become delirious with boredom, I walked downstairs and decided to make an omelet and tea for myself. Liz was working on her laptop amid piles of books on her desk. I opened the refrigerator to see if there were any eggs and saw two of them sitting in the door cabinet. I broke them open and started stirring them in a bowl. Just when I put the pan on the stove, I remembered Holly telling me that people should use their own groceries. I looked at Liz to ask if those eggs were hers. Before I said anything, she said, "Go ahead!" Although she seemed busy working, she knew what I was up to. Feeling guilty about using her eggs, I offered her tea, but she replied, "No thanks!" She said that in a way that suggested, "I am busy and please don't try to talk to me."

I had been in the United States for just a few days at the time and hadn't quite understood the idea of personal space. I walked up to her and started looking at the books she had on her desk. She continued typing and ignored my presence. As I browsed through the books, a strange object, among several other things on her desk, caught my attention. I dropped the book in my hand and looked at the object curiously. Liz stopped typing. I saw her eyes looking at me and then quickly shifting to what I was staring at. She frantically tried to stop me as I extended my arm to grab that eight inch long, two inch wide, pink shaft-like object. She reacted a little too slowly and I already had it my hand; Liz leaned back in her chair with an exasperated sigh and started typing again. It took me a few minutes of messing around with that thing to figure out that it was a replica of a man's penis. Bewildered by its presence on a study table, and in immediate need of an explanation, I looked at Liz. She looked at me from the corner of her eye and then quickly bent her head down like she was looking into her lap. Feeling disgusted, I quickly threw that hideous-looking thing back on the desk as if I had accidently grabbed a dead snake. I hurried upstairs and didn't come out of my room for the rest of the day. My attempt to socialize with Liz had come to a very sad end. We did not make eye contact for several days. After that incident, I made sure she wasn't home before I went downstairs to watch TV, drink a glass of water, or cook something for myself.

Keith's room was right next to mine. He always seemed to come to pick up some stuff and then quickly leave. I wanted to talk to him and he seemed friendly, but apart from a few hellos and an exchange of smiles, we didn't get to talk much. One day, when no one was home, I went down and made tea. I saw Keith sitting on the couch, watching TV. I asked him if he would like to try some Indian tea and he said, "I would love to." It was great to hear him say that. It was an encouraging answer. I brought an extra cup and sat down next to him. He told me he liked travelling and would like to go to India one day. Seeing him show interest in my country, I enthusiastically told him about all the good places to visit. After a few minutes he asked me, "Have you met your in-laws?"

I said, "Not yet, but I am going to visit Brockway soon. I will meet them for the first time then."

He removed his lips from the cup and looked at me as if he was going to say something. I waited for him to speak. He didn't say anything and took a sip from the cup.

I continued looking at him. "Are they nice?" he asked.

"I think so...I have talked to them on the phone... they seem to be nice," I said, "why do you ask?"

"My grandparents aren't nice...they don't like my mother."

"Why?"

"They are racist," he continued, "my mom is from Portugal and they don't consider her to be white."

After a few minutes of awkward silence, he said, "But I hope your wife's folks like you."

After finishing his tea, he thanked me for offering it to him and started leaving, but just before he shut the door behind him, he pointed a finger at me and said, "Don't let them give you a hard time."

A Walking Tour

~

One of my favorite pastimes in Lucknow was going for long walks. Although I walked at any time of the day, early mornings were especially good, since fewer people were out and about and the air was cleaner. Since my parents always lived in the heart of the city, where all the action was and all the important buildings were—mausoleums hundreds of years old, the historic British Residency and several other buildings built by the British, including the railway station and the post office—it was hard to find a quiet time to walk. I liked to leave early in the morning, and on my walk, I found rickshaw pullers sleeping on their cycle rickshaws, balancing their scrawny bodies between the handlebar and the seat, and families of construction workers sleeping inside makeshift huts made of loosely stacked bricks and tarpaulins, by the side of the road. It seemed as if the homeless people on the streets tried to make the best of the cool early morning breeze and enjoyed the last hour's sleep before they had to get up and toil under the scorching sun.

I usually walked to one particular mausoleum that had a cricket field in front of it. Oftentimes I found young boys playing cricket there. I sat on a five-foot brick wall that surrounded the field and watched them play. After enjoying the game for an hour—the boys sometimes invited me to play with them—I would stop for a cup of *chai* tea at a roadside stall across the street from the field, where some elderly folks, who were also morning walkers, gathered in a group and complained about their disobedient daughters-in-law and submissive sons who had become puppets to their wives. After having two or three glasses—each one no bigger than a test tube—of *chai*, I would take a longer route to walk back home and watch the city come alive—people rushing to work on their mopeds, daily wage laborers pedaling hard with a steel lunch box hanging from the handle bars of their bicycles, and cycle rickshaws carrying fifteen school children. If I found myself too far from home, I would take a shortcut to get back—I knew all the back roads.

A few days after I arrived in Charlottesville, I started getting an urge to explore the city on foot. I decided to discover the place on a beautiful afternoon in the month of September; leaves were falling on the ground, the breeze was gentle and the temperature was just right. Even though we lived near the University, I had seen very little of the campus—I decided to walk around the college and slowly work my way around town. As I walked towards the center of the campus, I saw young college students wearing expensive-looking shoes and backpacks, walking busily about. Every other person had earphones plugged into his or her ears and percussive music leaked through. I couldn't tell if they had them on because they couldn't walk without their favorite music or because they wanted to cut out the outside noise—which was non-existent.

I climbed up a hilly path to find myself looking down a set of circular steps carved in a ditch-like structure. About twenty big steps descended down in the bottom of the hill, in front of a cement platform. It appeared to be an open-air theater. The stage was empty, but a few students, mostly girls, were lying on the steps on towels, baring their backs, bathing in the sun. There were a couple of boys playing guitar. The place reminded me of the *ghats* in Varanasi, where tourists, pilgrims worshipping and feeding cows, and people getting their heads shaved dotted the entire length of steps on the banks of the river Ganges. When I spent time in Varanasi, several people came up to me selling massages, flowers, boat rides; hippie tourists sat around and smoked hashish, looking over the sacred Ganges, trying to feel spiritual, and some other long-haired white tourists played sitar and sang George Harrison's "My Sweet Lord." In Charlottesville, I sat down on the steps at the university for a few minutes. Although there was a stage at the bottom of the steps, there was nothing happening; the place was clean and quiet. Sitting there and looking around, I tried to imagine what the *ghats* in Varanasi would look like if all the mediating *sadhus* (ascetics), stalls selling marigolds, sweets, incense, and devotees performing rituals were not there.

I got up and started walking again. After a few minutes, I found myself on a narrow bridge above a railway track. Its boundary walls were painted black, blue, purple, and silver— so many times that the paint was peeling off in six inch thick layers. Slogans like, "GO HOOS" and "WAHOO" were sprayed on them. It seemed as if someone had emptied a giant tank full of paint on the boundary walls of the bridge. It was amazing to see people waste so much paint. I wandered away wondering why someone would do that.

After some time, it looked as if I had walked into a student residential area. The steps and the doors of the houses had Greek letters, and words painted on them, and every other house on that street seemed to be having a party. Loud music poured out as shirtless boys and skimpily dressed girls danced on the white wooden balconies of the brown brick houses. The sidewalks were littered with empty beer cans and pizza boxes. As I continued walking I heard Dave Matthews crooning somewhere, and saw some students playing Frisbee in front of a house.

After a few minutes of walking, I noticed the music and loud students were gone, the street was impeccably clean, and houses looked rich and majestic with big white columns supporting the balconies; the streets and driveways were crammed with shiny BMWs, Jaguars, and Mercedes.

Wandering aimlessly, admiring fine-looking bungalows, the greenery, and wondering about the opulence around the area, I turned a corner and found myself in a completely different neighborhood. Young black children—they seemed to be under ten years of age—crisscrossed with their tiny bicycles on the trash littered street; teen-aged boys stood around in groups wearing T-shirts four sizes bigger than their torsos and hats turned sideways. Houses were small and had shingles flaking off their roofs. 1970's-era huge cars with rust holes in them and paint peeling off sat in front of many houses; some of them had big shiny rims and the speakers rattled the whole car as they passed by, playing loud music. Sad-looking old black men with white beards sat on their front porches and followed me with their eyes until I was out of their sight. I did not see a single white person on that street. I came up to an intersection where I saw a barbershop, a convenience store, and a thrift store.

I paused to look into the barbershop and saw, through the big glass window, black customers getting their hair cut by black barbers. I walked into the convenience store to buy a drink. The cashier looked and spoke like me, but it turned out that he—he introduced himself as Roy—had never been to India; his parents were Indian, but he had lived in Kenya for most of his life, and had recently moved to the US. When I told him that I had just arrived in the US, he said, "Welcome to America!" I thanked him, and hung around to chat with him for a few minutes. His store was like a general merchant's shop in Lucknow that sells things of daily use, and can be found in almost every corner of the city. He sold cigarettes, little cupcakes, pastries, soap, and bottled water, but the most popular thing seemed to be the lottery ticket—I saw at least three out of four customers coming to enquire about the result. I also noticed that most of those people reeked of alcohol. While I was there, a tall, skinny, disheveled middle-aged black man walked into the store, opening the door with a loud thud. Wobbling on his feet, hanging on to the counter and the wall, he grabbed a case of beer and presented himself to Roy. Instead of taking his money, Roy pointed his finger in the customer's face and said, "Listen, I don't want any trouble, alright...I will lose my license if you keep doing this." He took the beer off the counter, and the drunkard walked out scratching his head, without saying anything. Surprised at Roy's behavior, I asked him what happened. Roy said, "It is illegal to sell alcohol to someone already drunk...and this guy has been drinking since 9 o'clock this morning." I talked to him for a few more minutes, and listened to him complain about his job and when I opened the door to leave, he said, "Be prepared to struggle. Life is not as easy in America as most people think."

I came out of his store and started walking again. Soon, I realized I had been walking for more than an hour. I crossed a few small intersections and tried to figure out where I was. In India, I generally located myself by remembering the shops, street stalls, a bright-colored temple, or a tall minaret of a mosque. Since most of the shops had different names and different looks, and I never saw two Hindu temples on one street that belonged to the same god, it was easy to find my way around. This is a problem in Charlottesville, as many of the convenience stores are called Seven-Eleven and there are plenty of them. Restaurants are all chain businesses and there is no way of telling one from the other. Unlike India, I found only two streets in Charlottesville that had any sign of life: the one with the students partying and the one where the kids were riding their bikes. Every other street was just like anywhere else—nondescript. One of the reasons why I liked walking in India was entertainment. I didn't have to go to a theatre to watch a play—a rickshaw puller fighting with his customer for an extra rupee, people dancing in a marriage procession in the middle of the street, and someone chasing down a shirtless boy who stole a loaf of bread from a bakery—there was enough drama to watch on the street. I didn't have to go to a stadium to watch a thrilling game of cricket—dads stopped their scooters and moms looked down from their balconies to see if their son could hit a six on the last ball of a match being played in the middle of an intersection. I didn't have to sit inside a cafeteria to have a cup of *chai*. The best things were available on the streets.

After walking quite a distance away from my home, I was disoriented. I didn't have a mobile phone to call my wife, but I knew I could ask someone where my street was. I wanted to walk some more in the hope that I might recognize where I was, so I continued. Some of the streets looked familiar, but I wasn't sure whether they were the ones that led to my home. After some time, I started looking around for a human face to ask directions. I didn't see any. I walked a little more in search of one.

After another fifteen minutes I still didn't see anyone. I found myself in a residential area where there were cars parked on both sides of the road and all the doors of the houses were shut. Not a soul could be seen. Every now and then a couple of cars would go by, but still not a person on foot. Knocking on someone's door didn't seem like an intelligent idea. I was hoping to see someone come out of his home so I could ask for help. I did see people leaving their homes, but they would start their car right inside their garage and open the door with a remote and drive away. It started getting dark, and I needed to get home.

Luckily, after some time I saw a woman coming out of one of the many houses. She was dressed in shorts, a sports bra, and sneakers. She stretched her arms and legs and started running in the opposite direction. I was surprised by how someone could be so skimpily dressed while I was bundled up to keep myself warm. By the time I stopped wondering, the girl had gotten a couple hundred meters away from me. Now I was left with two options: either try to run and chase her down or look for someone else to help me.

The first option sounded more sensible as the chances of finding another person seemed almost impossible. Now the challenge was to catch up with the girl who was wearing twenty times less clothing and was probably ten times more physically fit than me. Running uphill in a sweatshirt and heavy jeans and the wrong kind of shoes posed a daunting task. Hearing my heavy breathing and un-rhythmic footsteps—probably suspecting that I was following her—the girl doubled her speed. This was bad news for me. I was dying to get close to her and had covered less than half the distance. By increasing her speed, she reopened the gap between us, as if I hadn't run at all.

As I was trying to catch up with her, she kept getting farther and farther away. Not being able to run fast enough, I eventually lost her. She disappeared in the dark. In the process of running and trying to catch up with the girl, I stumbled upon a pedestrian street that had many fancy-looking stores on both sides—boutiques, gift shops, bookstores, and coffee shops. The whole length of the red-brick path had several leafy trees in the middle. There were outdoor stalls selling woolen hats, shawls, sunglasses, and other knickknacks. Street musicians sat against the walls and played flute, violin, and guitar. As people walked by, they stopped to drop a dollar or two in the hat or the guitar case that lay before the performers. Most were teenagers who seemed like they were just having a good time singing and playing their instrument, but some of them looked disheveled. One of them was playing harmonica. He was sitting on a bucket that was turned upside down and had a square cardboard box in front of him that had two lonely looking dollar bills in it. His long white hair mixed with light brown strands covered part of his face every time he blew his harp with an extra vigor. Since I enjoy playing harmonica myself, I stood there and listened to him for a while. I soon realized that I was getting distracted and went inside one of the coffee shops to ask for directions. The young woman behind the counter asked, "Hi, what can we get started for you?" I felt like telling her that I actually started three hours ago, I need to get finished now. I asked, "Could you please tell me how to get to Wiley Road?" She responded, "Sure…make a right out of here, and then turn left at the light, and then keep going straight through three lights, for about four miles…make a left at the hospital and you will find your street after a couple of blocks." I knew I had been walking for a long time but I didn't think I had gone as far as four miles from my home—there was something not right about her directions. It seemed to me that she had assumed that I was driving and left out the short cuts and one-way streets and told me a much longer way to get home. I asked another person who was sitting in his car in front of the coffee shop. He gave me exactly the same directions except for one difference—he told me to make the first turn left instead of right. I told the guy that the girl inside the shop told me make a right turn first, instead of going left. He said, "Yeah, she was right because you were inside the shop then." He started backing his car out and said, "Good luck!" As he left the parking lot, I stood there wondering what to do. I started walking again, following the directions given to me.

Being lost and asking directions brought to mind memories of our vegetable vendor, Gulab, in Lucknow, who pushed his cart full of fresh vegetables around town and claimed to know everyone and liked to help people who had gotten lost. He had a very distinct way of telling directions. If I asked him how to get somewhere, Gulab liked to question who exactly I wanted to meet and when I told him who it was, he asked why I wanted to meet that person. After he found out all the details—although it was none of his business—he got quiet for a few minutes and sprinkled water on his vegetables or counted his money, pretending I wasn't there. When I asked him again, he told me to wait, gesturing with his palm, and continued counting his dirty wet rupees. After a couple of minutes, he would start to tell me that he had been in that area a few years ago. On asking again if knew how to get there, he gave me vague directions. Seeing the impatience building up on my face and realizing that he had wasted my time, he frantically stopped a passing rickshaw driver and asked him about the address that I had asked him about twenty minutes before.

The two people whom I had spoken to in Charlottesville had very different ways of giving directions. They were quick, to the point, didn't want to know why I was going to Wiley road, and started me right where I was standing and—unlike India where directions given by two different people never match—their routes would have been identical if I hadn't moved two feet away from the girl. I reached home without any problem. My wife was waiting for me. I told her I had a lot to tell her about where I had been and what I had seen. She enthusiastically told me, "I just put the kettle on the stove—let's have tea and talk about what you have been up to."

A Trip to the Post Office

∾

After arriving in America, I started emailing my brother and friends about my life in the new country. Since my parents aren't computer literate, I had promised them I would write letters and send pictures via regular mail. So I needed to buy some stamps from a post office in Charlottesville.

For almost all my life in Lucknow, I used the General Post Office—commonly known as the GPO—for all my communication purposes. Surrounded by acres of well-kept gardens—a popular hangout for young lovers and for my friends to play cricket, or to just sit and talk on one of its many stone benches—it is one of the most beautiful buildings in the city. It has been a landmark for the residents of Lucknow—the sound of rickshaw drivers shouting "GPO, GPO, GPO, GPO," still echoes in my head—for as long as I can remember, and its clock tower is visible from miles away. If I wanted to watch a movie or just hang out with my friends, I would always gather with them at the GPO and then venture out into the town. It was more than just a post office for me.

Something that really sticks out among my memories of going to the GPO was going there to make phone calls with my friend A.J. The GPO had four old-style dial payphone booths and one of them was always busy with my friend who used it to call his girlfriend; a public phone was much safer than his own home where his parents' prying eyes could have found out about his love affair. There were other public phones in the town which were more private than the one in the GPO, but he preferred this one because it only required a one-rupee coin and let him talk as long as he wanted. He did a good job of continuing to smile and say sweet things on the phone while seven people around him waited for their turn with frowning faces. When I went to the GPO with him, I often left him there and ran errands—went to the bank, had a cup of coffee, spent some time in the library and came back after an hour and a half to find him still glued to the phone. I often thought my friend misused government property by talking for so long for just a rupee, but one time I saw someone even more crafty who used a rupee coin with a string glued to it and pulled it back out of the machine after he was done talking.

Apart from the payphones, the place provided other services like any other post office in town, but because of its central location, it was always the busiest. I remember being in line, jostling with forty other people, waiting to get to the counter. I can't forget the hustle and bustle and the smell of glue, the loud thump echoing off the walls every time the clerks stamped a letter, and the flutter of the pigeons flying inside the building, from one corner to the other.

When I set out to go to a post office in Charlottesville, I had no idea what to expect. I walked to the nearest post office and saw a nondescript building that said, "United States Postal Service." I opened the glass door—it had two panels, one said "Enter" and the other "Do Not Enter." It didn't make any sense to me. In a country where the literacy rate is almost hundred percent, people should be able to use their common sense and figure out which door to use, especially when both of them lead to one small cubicle. I also wondered how big of an offense it would be if I used the "Do Not Enter," panel to enter.

Growing up with some mischievous friends, I sometimes indulged in doing the opposite of what the signs said—peed where it said, "Do Not Urinate Here," spat where it said, "Don't Spit Here," and parked where it said, "Don't Park Here". I had the urge to do so at the post office and go through the wrong gate, but I followed the instructions. I walked in and saw people waiting in line. There was an ATM-type machine in one corner of the room. One young lady walked in and stuck her credit card into it and the device spat out a strip of stamps, making sounds like *bizeet bizeet*. She was in and out in less than two minutes. Like her, I just needed stamps and could have used the machine instead of waiting in line, but I was too intimidated by the apparatus to use it. The flashing lights and the colorful buttons seemed too daunting. I decided to get in the queue and do things the old-fashioned way; talking to someone in person and telling him what I wanted seemed easier than interacting with a computerized machine.

The post office had low ceilings and the floor was linoleum. It didn't have any kind of smell, or at least I didn't notice any; it looked sterile. The only sounds that I could hear were of fingers tapping on keyboards and receipts printing on a printer. Every now and then someone walked in and grabbed an envelope or a box—there was a blue colored wooden rack against the wall that had different sized envelopes piled up on it—that suited their item. I noticed that some of the envelopes had plastic bubbles to protect the delicate items and there was a paper strip attached inside that revealed the glue after being detached. I remembered the guy in Lucknow who sat on the sidewalk outside the post office and sold envelopes and packed people's stuff for a charge. He stuffed in newspapers and dried grass to provide extra padding and then stitched the opening of the jute bags that he used; he could pack anything, it didn't matter how small, delicate, or big it was. Sitting by the side of the road on a small wooden stool, he did good business because the post office did not provide any packaging service. I often saw foreign tourists patiently waiting to get their books or an Indian drum set packed.

The post office in Charlottesville seemed to be a serious place. Three employees, two men and one woman, wore blue uniforms, a monogram on their shirts and a stern look on their faces—they didn't seem to smile at all. The line of people waiting for their turn was orderly, and no one was trying to cut in, shove, or yell. While I was observing everything and noticing the differences, I realized that there was a huge gap between each person waiting in line—at least four or five feet; it was enough for a scooter to go through. I have driven my scooter through narrower passages in India.

The post office was not a huge place and the big gap in the line was causing people to stand near the exit door, almost pushing them out of the building. I had never seen this before. In India, I don't remember—ever—having more than six inches between me and the next person standing in line whether I was buying stamps at the post office, getting tickets to watch a movie or getting on a train. A lot of times I found it easier to have people so close to one other—especially when I had to get on a train. All I had to do was to position myself at a spot where my train compartment was supposed to stop. The rest was done by the hundred other passengers behind me who literally lifted me up and plunked me on the train. The same was the case when I had to get off. People were so tightly packed that I often lost my footing and if my glasses got displaced, my hands—stuck in someone's armpit or crushed between two huge bellies—couldn't reach to fix them. I found myself moving forward without my feet touching the ground. If I left more than a foot gap between me and the next person, people assumed I wasn't in line and the next thing I knew that there was another person in line in front of me.

When I saw people standing so far apart at the post office in Charlottesville, it didn't make any sense to me. I couldn't help myself and moved closer to the guy in front. He immediately turned back and looked at me and moved a couple of paces ahead, re-opening the gap between me and him. I didn't understand what made him move. I thought I had left enough room between me and him; it must have been more than a foot. I turned back and saw the person behind me hadn't moved closer to me even when I had shifted away from him. It seemed to me as if he wasn't in line at all—he was that far away. While I stood there and waited, a middle-aged lady walked in and went to a customer—who was not in line and writing something on a package, leaning on a table—and asked, "Are you in line, sir?"

He replied, "Oh no, I am on my way out."

The lady smiled and got into the line and said, "Just making sure." I stood there and watched everything in amazement. It all seemed strange to me. I was puzzled by everyone's behavior. I moved a couple of steps again and got closer to the guy ahead. This time he turned back and gave me a stern look and moved away. I was very confused and wanted to know what I was doing wrong. I extended my arm and put my hand on his shoulder gently and asked, "Am I causing you any trouble?" He jerked my hand off his shoulder and left the post office in a hurry. I didn't know what had angered him and looked at the guy behind me to see his reaction. He curled his lips and strained his eyebrows. Standing there clueless, I heard the clerk say, "Can I help the next person in line?" It was my turn. I presented myself to the guy behind the counter who had an earring in one ear, and the only hair on his head was a red goatee. A burly guy, he had his head shaved and, to me at that moment, seemed to have the face of a psycho serial killer. He reminded me of a baddie in an Indian movie.

He asked me, "How can I help you?" I had an envelope to send to India so I showed it to him and asked how much it would cost. He looked at it and asked me to pay 42 cents. I bought some stamps and left the place, surprised at how cheap it was to mail the letter to India. Also, I wanted to tell the clerk that he was wasting his time stamping people's envelopes behind the counter in a mind-numbing atmosphere and that he should go to Mumbai and try his luck as an actor. There are lots of film producers scoping out the upscale bars and nightclubs of India's financial capital for white tourists to play some role in their film.

I came out of the post office and started walking back, whistling my favorite Hindi song, and I noticed someone looking at me strangely and then suddenly changing his course of direction. I paused to take another look—I realized it was the guy who had been ahead of me at the post office.

The next day, the postman came to my home and delivered some letters. There was one envelope which appeared to have my handwriting on it. Interestingly, it was the same letter that I had mailed the day before. I told the postman it was supposed to go to India and not be delivered back to me. He looked at the address and pointed out that I had written the "to be delivered address" where the "return address" was supposed to be. It would have been okay in India, but I learned that in the U.S., the "sender" is mentioned on the top left corner of the envelope and the "recipient" goes at the bottom right.

I found out why it only cost forty-two cents to mail that letter.

Haircut

~

A few days before I was going to meet my in-laws in Brockway, Holly suggested I should get my hair cut. Since I was going to visit her family for the first time, she thought, it would be a good idea to look respectable. I knew haircuts were expensive in America and my money was tight, so I had waited as long as I could. Since my hair grows quickly I had to get it trimmed every month—sometimes sooner than that—back in India, but I didn't go to a barber for three months in Charlottesville. My hair was beginning to take a wild shape. I procrastinated as long as I could, but, eventually, I gave up and she dragged me to the nearest hair-cutting salon.

I was going to get my hair cut for the first time in the US, and didn't know what to expect. I asked Holly—thinking that she might know because she had her hair cut in both countries—if she knew anything about getting a haircut in America, and if it was any different from India. She said,

"The only thing I can tell you is that unlike India, you have to tip your hairdresser here…but other than that I won't be able to tell you what it is like from a man's perspective," she looked at me helplessly, "my hair is a lot longer than yours, and I don't have to get my sideburns trimmed."

In India, I used to go to a barbershop that was run by an elderly gentleman. His shop was always busy with people sitting on a long bench reading a local newspaper, or listening to news on an old crackly sounding transistor radio—I once asked how old it was, and he said he had gotten it as a wedding gift twenty-five years ago—that was held together by several rubber bands. The walls of his shop were covered with calendars of Hindu gods and goddesses and the ceiling had a fan that produced more noise than air. Everyone waited patiently for their turn and some people who were in a hurry popped their heads into his shop and asked, "How long?" Continuing to concentrate, and without looking up, he responded, "Come back in an hour."

He was half-bald and wore thick black-framed eyeglasses, and always chewed a *paan*, betel nut and tobacco wrapped in a leaf that made a lump in his mouth and made the corners of his lips red. While cutting hair, he would stop several times to step out of the shop and spit. I never had to tell him what to do. He always knew how I wanted my hair cut or how he thought my hair should be cut; there was no arguing with him, and he always sent me home satisfied. A meticulous worker, he made sure everyone got a perfect haircut, even if it took more than an hour for the job. Sometimes he let his son cut his customers' hair and as part of the training, he occasionally gave a wallop on his head if he messed up. My parents told me that he had been cutting my hair since I was four years old. My family moved a couple of times, but we were always in the vicinity of his shop. Over the period of several years, he had raised his price from five to twelve rupees. Even at twelve rupees, the price was around a quarter of a dollar.

I was nervous when I went for my first haircut in Charlottesville. It was a swank place with mirrors covering every inch of the walls and windows festooned with bottles of shampoo, lotions, and various other products for hair care. Since I had never had a woman cut my hair, it troubled me to see only female employees in the salon. A young lady, wearing a black miniskirt and a deep-necked sleeveless top at the front desk was taking people's names and giving them a number. She had blond hair and a shiny silver piece of metal stuck out every time she opened her mouth.

I took a number and watched other people while I waited for my turn. The place catered to both male and female customers. About fifteen minutes later, someone called, "Deepak" in a tone that matched my wife calling me when she wants me to do something that I hate. I felt awkward. I rose from my chair and said, "Yes, it's me."

She said, "Alright, follow me, honey!" I had never had anyone else other than my wife call me honey. I turned my head around to check if she was talking to somebody else.

"I'm talking to you, honey. It's your turn," she said, looking at me with a cheeky smile. I looked at my wife, asking for permission with my eyes to go with the girl, and hesitantly started walking towards her. She made me sit down on a very comfortable revolving black chair, and covered me with a shiny black robe. I could see in the mirror that she had long eyelashes—they didn't look natural—and her finger nails were painted dark brown. She asked me, "So, what are we doing today?" I wondered how obvious I had to make it for her to understand that I was there for a haircut. I mean, I was in a haircutting salon, sitting on a chair in front of a mirror with shabby looking hair. What else we could be doing? I gave her a curious look and said, "Just a haircut."

"I know, honey, but what would you like to be done to your hair?" she said, while running her long fingers through my oily, and probably dirty, hair. She pointed towards a wall of pictures of men with different hair styles and said, "Do you want to look like one of those guys?"

One of the guys in the picture had a three inch high, and half inch wide patch of hair running across his head. It was like a bushy fence in the middle of a football field with nothing on either side. Another guy had extremely short hair in the front, but foot-long hair in the back of his head. It seemed as if he jumped off the chair in the middle of the haircut and never returned, leaving the job unfinished. The third guy had a big puff on the top off his head, quite like Elvis'.

I wondered what my parents would think if I showed up at their door with any of these hairstyles. My father is very fussy about one's hair and he does not like people who have untidy hair. He was one of the reasons why I never changed my barber in India; he inspected my head after every haircut, walking round me in a full circle to make sure the hair was neatly trimmed around my ears, my sideburns weren't too long, and that it was short enough to suit his taste. Once I went to a different barber—one that had electric razors and comfortable chairs—and when I tried to sneak inside the house, hoping he wouldn't notice, he pulled me aside, yanking at my shirtsleeve, and asked me to turn around so he could take a look at my head. He looked down, and then looked into my eyes in a way that meant I had hugely disappointed him. It felt as if he had caught me cheating on my wife or something equally bad. "You must have gotten your hair cut by someone else this time," he said. I didn't say anything. He told me to go back to my old barber the same day to get it fixed.

My father had instilled in me the habit of keeping my hairstyle conventional. I didn't want my hair to look like any of those people on the wall. I told the lady I wanted my hair to look respectable. "Sure honey, I will use a number two razor," she said, and took my glasses off, holding them carefully between her index finger and thumb, and put them away. It felt awkward because everything she was doing was quite like my wife, calling my name in a flattering way, running her fingers through my hair, and taking my glasses off, as my wife does when I fall asleep reading a book. I was nervous because a woman was cutting my hair, and now that my glasses were gone—it always feels awkward if a stranger taking my glasses off—I felt vulnerable; it's worse than taking my clothes off in public. I sat docilely, enshrouded in a black cloth, in front of a skimpily dressed woman who was going to change the way I looked. It was scary.

In the mirror, I saw two white hands mercilessly stripping hair off my scalp with an electric razor. My hair was rolling down my face in the shape of small balls. I had never seen that happen to me before. With every swing of her hand, down came a big lump. Every couple of minutes the lady slid both hands down my cheeks to turn my head in a certain direction to get the right angle for her razors. After running the shaver in all directions on my head she was done, in less than ten minutes. She grabbed my glasses and put them back on my nose and swiveled the chair towards the mirror.

"Whaddya think, honey?" she asked.

I curiously looked to see if the person in the mirror was me. My face was very different a few minutes ago. She had cut my hair very short which made my face look extra round and chubby. I was disappointed, but I didn't want to take any risk and cause more damage by asking the lady to fix it. I said, "It's good."

"Alrighty, I was hoping you would say that," she swiveled my chair back towards the mirror, "let me clean you up and we will be all set." She started blowing air in my ears, in my face, and around my neck with some shotgun-like apparatus that sounded like someone was trying to put air in their car tire. She was trying to blow away the little bits of hair that were stuck in and around my face, but she didn't realize that by blowing air in my face she was actually sending the tiny bits of hair deep inside my ears and my nose.

She turned off the air pump device and asked me, "Would you like me to shampoo your hair, honey?" I had had enough of her so I said, "No, thanks!"

"Okay," she said, and took the robe off and asked me to come to the reception counter. I followed her, and she asked me to pay $14. It was a large sum of money for an awful haircut. Standing there, I quickly did the math in my head and realized it would buy me more than seventy haircuts from my barber in India. It also made me think that my barber would have to cut seventy people's hair—and spend a long time since he didn't use electric razors—to make $14. I had never given such a serious thought to a haircut before. While signing the bill, I noticed she looked up but kept her eyes fixed on the line between the amount and the total on the bill. I remember my wife telling me about tipping my hair dresser. I resentfully gave her three dollars for giving me a bad haircut and blowing all the dirty loose hair in my face. She thanked me and said, "See you soon, honey." In the span of nine minutes she had called me honey at least ten times—that's more than my wife does in a month. I immediately decided I wouldn't see her again and left the place.

A few days later, Raja, an Indian friend of mine came to visit us in Charlottesville from a suburb of Washington, DC. He asked me to take him to a barber where he could get his head shaved as part of a Hindu ritual that follows the death of a family member. Although I had decided I would never go back to the same place I had gotten my hair cut, my wife suggested we give them another chance. She said this time we couldn't go wrong since my friend needed his head shaved—the odds of getting a bad haircut were almost zero. Raja agreed with Holly, and we went back to the same place. His turn came soon after arriving there. I started flipping through a magazine, thinking that it would take him a while since his whole head needed to be shaved. I knew it took a long time when I got mine done in India. Interestingly, Raja came back in less than ten minutes. All his hair was gone but something didn't look right, and he looked unhappy. After spending fourteen dollars, and ten minutes at the salon, we discovered that my friend's head was actually not shaved to suit him. The hair was cut very close to the skin, but not shaved bald. The Hindu ritual required the kind of shave that took shaving cream and a razor, and not the kind that electric clippers produced.

After that incident, I decided to look for a male barber in town, and found a barbershop run by an older white gentleman named Tom. He was broad-shouldered, square-jawed, white-haired, and more than six feet tall. His shop looked old with plaster peeling off the facade and paint flaking off the squeaky wooden door. He had half a dozen chairs, a coat rack, and a few magazines that were strewn across the coffee table in his shop; the shiny brown wooden walls were ringed with pictures of his family. Although there were three hair-cutting stations, Tom was the only barber.

When I went to get my hair cut, I opened the door and saw him cutting hair. As I walked in, he stopped cutting and looked at me. I looked at him and said, "I am here to get my hair cut." He replied, "You got money?"

Surprised at his question, I said, "Of course!"

"Alright then, I'll cut your hair," he said, and burst into laughter along with three other customers. I sat down on a chair. Most of the customers looked to be around fifty years of age, and they seemed to know Tom well. They joked with him and he joked back. I asked one of the customers sitting next to me about how long had he been coming to Tom's. He said, "Ever since I was ten."

"That's a long time!"

"Yep, Tom is a good guy and every time I come here I meet my buddies."

I said, "Oh, okay!"

Another person sitting next to me said, "Gossip ain't bad here," and started laughing.

Tom bent his head down and looked above his reading glasses and said, "And most of the time it's true." Bob had a good sense of humor and seemed to enjoy what he was doing. My turn came and I sat down on his chair. As he started cutting my hair he said, "You got a lotta hair, young man." I said, "I used to have more."

"You still got plenty...my wife would love me if I had this much hair." He laughed and then asked, "Where are you from?"

"India."

"Every once in a while I get some international students from the university."

"Oh, okay," I said, "do you ever have problems communicating with them?"

"Not really, but one time a Chinese guy came and said he wanted his hair cut short," Tom paused and took a couple of steps back to face me and continued with the story, "I started cutting but after a few minutes he started jumping out of the chair...I kept pulling him back and he kept jumping out of the chair...I didn't speak any Chinese and he didn't speak English." He started laughing out loud.

I asked him, "What happened in the end?"

"Well, I cut his hair, but he thought it was too short."

Although Tom didn't speak Hindi, the radio was tuned to a bluegrass music station instead of All India Radio, the pictures on the wall weren't calendars of Indian gods and goddesses, and the customers in the shop were all white, he reminded me of my barber in India. I felt comfortable and he charged me only half as much as the other place in Charlottesville. I knew I would go back to him.

Eating Out

～

One of the things I started missing right after coming to America was being able to have *chai* on the street. In India, I used to stop by roadside tea stalls and have *chai* several times a day. My favorite *chai-wallah* was a middle-aged man named Ramesh. His stall—a green wooden cart on four wheels—was situated under a sprawling *peepal* tree. He made the best *chai* in town. There was nothing like watching him prepare it; He swirled the pan two inches above the gas-canister stove every time the froth rose to the brim and then he set it down and let it spill over and sizzle onto the burner. The spicy froth created an aroma as it spilled over the hot stove with a hissing sound. The smell of ginger, cardamom, sugar and tea boiling together reminded me of him and made me walk to his stall craving *chai*. I was addicted to the sweet taste of milky tea mixed with spices.

Ramesh provided more than just that *chai*. His stall was a meeting place for my friends. We would gather around his cart and discuss why India lost a recent cricket match or which political party would win in the next election. Ramesh also acted as our weather channel—he had a great sense of when it would rain or how hot it would be in the near future. He always opened his shop at five in the morning and closed at ten in the night. No matter what day of the week it was, Ramesh was there, boiling tea under the tree.

One day in Charlottesville, I craved *chai*, and decided to find its equivalent in my new country. I walked to a cafeteria housed in a students' bookstore on the university campus. After looking around the bookstore for a while, I decided to get a cup of coffee. The cafeteria was nothing more than a huge glass counter against a wall. It had a big board hanging on the wall displaying the names of various drinks—mocha, macchiato, café latte, hot chocolate, iced coffee, iced tea, etc.

I looked at the board for a few minutes and tried to find hot tea—it wasn't there. Since I had never had most of the displayed drinks and didn't know what they were, I went to the counter and looked for the attendant. I looked to the left and to the right and craned my neck to see behind the counter but there was no one guarding that place. While I scratched my head and wondered what to do, I saw a small sign next to the cash register, "Be Back in 15 Minutes." I waited for a few minutes and then a short lady wearing a black hat and an apron, appeared. I asked, "Do you sell tea here?" The attendant said, "We have coffee." I decided to go for coffee and asked her,

"Can I have a cup of coffee?" She questioned, "Do you want regular coffee?" I didn't know what she meant by regular coffee and wondered what irregular coffee—if there was such a thing at all—would look like. To be on the safe side, I agreed to try the regular coffee. $1.74 was my total. She took my money and handed me an empty disposable cup. I looked at her and assumed that she was going to pour some coffee in it, but she turned around and started mopping the floor. I stood there for a few minutes helplessly, wondering what to do with that empty cup. After a little while, she noticed I was still there and pointed her finger towards the other side of the counter, "Oh, coffee is around the corner." I looked around and saw three thermos-type things with a nozzle attached to each of them. They had names such as, Decaf Expresso Valeroso, Santa Decosta Rica Bold, and French Roast. I wasn't familiar with any of them and wasn't sure if they were coffee. I looked at the dispensers wondering how to get coffee out of them.

I heard someone say, "Push the cap down!" Feeling embarrassed and totally lost I pushed the cap down, but in a state of confusion, I did not place my cup under the nozzle. As I pushed the cap down, a black colored hot liquid squirted out from the nozzle and spilled on the floor. I heard some snorting sounds in the background as if someone was trying to drink water through his nose. The cafeteria lady came running with a cloth and mopped the floor clean. I apologized for my ignorance. I tried again with my cup under the nozzle and filled my cup. Now my cup was filled with black liquid that smelled like an armpit. Its taste—it was like drinking sewer water—reminded me of the revolting syrup that my mother gave me when I got sick as a child. I asked the lady if I could get some milk so I could make it a little more tolerable. She pointed me to another corner of the cafeteria which had three smaller thermoses and several small blue, pink, and yellow colored sachets, stacked up lids for coffee cups, little packets of jelly, plastic utensils, and lots of paper napkins.

I poured the milk out of one of the flasks and opened a small sachet that said sugar. It took twenty minutes and lots of drama to get a small cup of coffee that tasted horrible. I wondered why they couldn't just give a ready-made cup of coffee to people and send them on their way. Why put people like me through such an ordeal? I could have used a step-by-step guide to buying a cup of coffee.

Getting a cup of coffee in India never involved seventeen steps. I asked for a coffee, and I got coffee—with frothy milk and sugar, in a china cup, ready to drink. No fancy names, no running around in circles.

On another occasion, when I was wandering aimlessly in Charlottesville, I found myself on a sidewalk with many restaurants. Almost every restaurant had a few chairs placed outside for people to sit and enjoy their meals in the beautiful September weather. Young college students sat around casually with their backs lazily leaning against the backrests and their bottoms perched on the edges of their chairs. Boys had their sunglasses on and hats backwards. Girls were dressed in halter tops, running their fingers through their hair, soaking in the sun and the cool breeze, with their armpits wide open to the sky. They sat around circular tables made of wrought iron which had plates with the remains of food—mostly bits of lettuce, tomatoes, and bread crumbs. I started to feel hungry and decided to have something to eat. I walked into a store which had an imposing picture of a sandwich—fifty times as big as a real sandwich—displayed on its window. As soon as I opened the door, the person behind the counter asked, "What can we get you, sir?"

I was a little taken aback as I didn't even have a chance to look at the menu or read through the hundred items painted on the wall. Prompted by the question, I told him I wanted a sandwich.

He asked, "What kind?"

Not sure, what I wanted, I asked, "What do you recommend?"

"Depends what you like."

This was my first experience buying a sandwich in the States and I did not have a clue what to order. So, I replied, "Why don't you pick one for me?"

"Do you like turkey?"

"Sure!" I said, pretending that I knew what turkey was.

"What kind of bread?"

I gave him an apologetic look that said, "I am sorry, I have no idea what you are asking."

I said, "Pick one."

He picked out some kind of bread for me and asked, "What kind of cheese do you want?"

Once again, I gave him a simple-minded look.

At this point, people behind me started getting restless.

"Sorry?" I said, thinking this hell was not over yet.

"Dude…" someone among fifteen people waiting behind me said. "Why don't you step aside and make up your mind…I gotta get back to work."

I walked out of the store feeling embarrassed.

I discovered that Charlottesville had more than four hundred restaurants, more than I had visited in my entire life. I was amazed to see that such a small city—with less than forty thousand people—could support so many food businesses. No matter what time of the day, week, or year, restaurants seemed to be full of people eating away. I often saw young moms and dads eating pizza while their little kids sat in high wooden chairs with tomato ketchup smeared on their faces. And when mom and dad wanted to dine with wine, the kids stayed home with the babysitter. Grey-haired men and women, sipping wine from classy goblets filled the large glass windows of expensive restaurants.

In India, it always had to be a special occasion for me to dress up and go out with my friends or family to a restaurant. Eating out was never an alternative to eating at home; it was a treat.

After faltering a few times, I realized that it was getting harder and harder to learn the skill of ordering food and not making myself look stupid. I let my wife order food for us when we decided to eat out. It wasn't that I couldn't tell the wait staff what I wanted, but what I really dreaded was not being able to answer the questions that followed right after I picked something from the menu. For instance, if I asked for, say, a pizza, the person waiting on me would immediately ask what kind of toppings I wanted. Now, you would think that it shouldn't be that hard, but I never knew what choices of toppings I had. After getting past that hurdle, came the question of what I wanted on the side. I would quickly say I didn't want anything, hoping the waiter or waitress would go away and bring my pizza. But it wouldn't stop here. Sides came with pizza, free, the wait staff would add. Since I didn't know my choices, I would be stumped once again. It was too much trauma for a simple meal.

I made more mistakes when I was faced with a skimpily dressed waitress who made an extra effort to please you by sounding like a flatterer—yeeeaah!—ofcourse!—surrre!— what can I do for ya?—and moved in every possible way to exhibit her body.

The waitress often wore a sleeveless top that showed her entire midriff and a skirt that started four inches below the belly button—which more likely than not would be pierced or have some hideous tattoo that involved an arrow pointing south—and stopped right after the crotch, exposing her full legs. I often found myself speechless when I encountered a voluptuous waitress—wearing a dress that was only slightly bigger than the napkin on my table—who asked me if I wanted to have tender breasts or well-done thighs. I found it disturbing.

In Lucknow, there were two restaurants where I ate most of the time. One was a hundred-year-old place called *Chowdhary's*—it was a fast food sit down restaurant that mostly sold snacks and sweets. It was built in a shape of a train compartment—long and narrow. I liked it because it was cheap—a couple of *samosas*, fried cutlets and a *Pepsi* cost less than twenty rupees, about fifty cents—and the service was fast; it was a good place to stop for a quick meal. The place used to be so busy that the waiters didn't have time to be nice to anyone; they threw the menu on the table as they walked by in a hurry to serve someone else. I often had to raise my arm, snap my fingers, shout, or even tug at their sleeves as they whizzed past me, carrying three dishes in each hand, a towel on the shoulder, and a bunch of crumpled rupees sticking out from the shirt pocket. A few minutes after serving the food, if they saw a pause in my eating, they would assume I was finished. If I looked away for a second or if they saw my Coke bottle three quarters empty, a waiter would swing by and stick a finger in and take it away. I often had to wrestle with them—hold the bottle down as they picked it up and tried to pull it out of my hands.

The other place I visited was called Kwality—an upscale eatery where shiny silverware adorned the neatly placed red and white checkered tablecloths on large rosewood tables; the waiters wore a dark brown buttoned-down jacket and matching pants as uniform. Oftentimes, there were more waiters than customers. I felt intimidated when three waiters walked towards me the minute I opened the restaurant's door—all of them competing with each other to get me. The place was often empty because of their high prices and I only went there when someone else was paying. The waiters served food promptly, filled my glass with water immediately after I took a swig, stood there with hands folded behind their back, and stared at my table looking for another opportunity to fill my glass or pour gravy from the vessel onto my dish. I would give them a wry smile and hope they would leave. They would stand there and continued to gawk.

In Charlottesville, every time I walked by a Taco Bell, McDonalds, Burger King, or any other fast food eatery I noticed that there wasn't anyone inside the restaurant, but the whole building would be encircled by cars, SUVs, and pick-up trucks. People patiently sat on four wheels covered by two tons of metal for a long time and moved a couple of inches every ten minutes towards the food window. Once I went through the drive-thru thinking it would be quick, but it took—I timed it—thirty-seven minutes. I had to turn off my car engine at least three times to cover a distance of less than thirty feet. It was excruciatingly slow.

One day, my wife and I set out on a late evening stroll. After walking for an hour or so, we got hungry. Since we were already out and tired from walking, we decided to eat at a fast food restaurant which happened to be on our way home. We went to the door and tried opening it but an employee from inside—who was mopping the floor—gestured with his hands to tell us that the restaurant was closed and that we should use the drive-thru which was still open.

Since we were on foot, we decided to walk to the drive-thru. We stood in front of the giant food screen that had a sensor to detect vehicles as they cruised up to it. Since we were not in a car, we did not get any response from the speaker mounted near the screen. I waved my hands, moved my legs up and down, and jumped in front of the screen—hoping it would detect some action. It didn't. Since our bodies were not as big as any car, I decided to turn my backside—which is a little rounder than other parts of my body—towards the screen and performed a little butt-shake dance. Still no response. A little flustered, we walked up to the food window and asked if we could get some food using the drive-thru service. A guy with headphones slid the window open and told us (assuming we were stupid and parked our car in the parking lot and came to the window on foot) that we needed to get in our car and then come. When we told him that we did not have our car with us, he looked at us as if we were the most simple-minded people he ever met. He told us he couldn't help us without the car. He said the device on the screen is linked with the computer inside the restaurant that generates orders after detecting a vehicle. We needed to be inside a metal box for the computer to give commands to the waiters to provide us with some food that—I was sure at this point—would contain every employee's spit.

We walked home without eating.

Getting Sick

~

My mother always acted as an in-house doctor for me, my two siblings and my father. She had an answer for most of our health problems—diarrhea, headaches, fever, sore throat, toothache—and her homemade remedies usually worked. If her medicines didn't do the job, she would get us antibiotics; she saved all the prescriptions from her previous visits to the doctor and referred to them every time her family got sick. Since she didn't have any medical training, doctors often scolded her for doing so. I only remember one bad incident of her self-medication; she gave me a pill that was a size of a bullet to cure my stomach disorder and as a result of the side effect, my body, almost immediately, turned pink and started itching severely. A lot of times, we just closed our eyes and gulped down the thoroughly ground mixture of spices—it was often basil, ginger, black pepper and honey—in her little pot, no matter how bitter it tasted. We knew it would make us feel better the next day, and it did.

She not only treated us when we got sick, but also, constantly, warned us to not do things that would make us sick. "Don't roam around the house without slippers," "don't eat street food," "don't play in the dirt," "don't go out in the cold without a jacket and a hat," were some of her most common orders and when we disregarded them and ate street food, went out in the cold with not enough clothes and got sick, she would yell, "I told you…but you never listen to me."

Living with her for thirty years, I got conditioned to her way of living and doing things. When I first arrived in Charlottesville, the September weather felt cold to me and reminded me of my mother. Although she was ten thousand miles away, I could hear voice clearly in my head; I made sure I wore enough clothes to protect myself from getting sick. After a few days, I noticed that I was the only one wearing a jacket and a scarf while everyone else was in shorts and t-shirts. I felt self-conscious. I decided to take my jacket off and walk around wearing a light shirt. I roamed the streets and enjoyed the cool breeze and realized it was not all that cold and that I was wearing heavy clothes because my mother had taught me to do so—not because I was feeling cold.

After a few days of enjoying the cooler weather, I developed a cold. Initially, I thought it was just an ordinary headache, but I didn't know it was there to stay for a long time. I sneezed incessantly and my nostrils were blocked for more than a month. Not being able to breathe, I stayed up most nights. I don't remember a common cold giving me so much trouble at any other time in my life. My stuffy nose caused my voice to become nasal—it was like speaking with my nose stapled shut. I limited my phone conversations with my mother because I feared she might find out that I was sick by listening to my voice. I didn't want her to worry—especially when she couldn't be there to help—and kept telling her that the phone sounded crackly or the line was not clear. My excuses for not talking to her long enough didn't last very long; I finally told her of my illness. After a long pause she asked what I had done to get sick. I knew it would upset her if I told her about not wrapping up well enough and being careless in the colder climate. I had already been hiding my illness for long enough and felt bad about it. I decided to tell her the truth. She got quiet and didn't speak for a minute. When I asked if she was still there, she gave me a long lecture and made me promise her that I would not do this again.

Since she couldn't send me her homemade medicine, she suggested that I should inhale steam with some nasal decongestant in it. I followed her advice and started inhaling steam several times a day. I didn't care what other members of the house thought of me ducking my face in a bowl with my head covered with a towel. The house smelled like medicine. I started feeling better soon. But due to constant wiping and rubbing I developed a pimple; it was right at the tip of my nose and hurt every time I sneezed, laughed, or shook my head heartily. I waited for it to go away, but it didn't. Instead, it got bigger and grew pink in color—causing me to be in agony and to wear an expression that always looked distressed.

When the pain became unbearable, I walked to the nearest pharmacy and presented my nose to a gentleman with a long white coat and wild white hair. I asked him, "Could you tell me what has happened to my nose?" He bent his head down, slid his reading glasses down his nose with his index finger, and peered through the gap between his forehead and specs and said, "It seems to be a pimple—a big one!"

"What do I do to get rid of it?"

"You need some antibiotics…"

I felt optimistic and asked, "How much are those?"

"Ten to fifteen dollars…"

I thought fifteen dollars was a very small price to get rid of the small volcano that was sitting an inch away from eyes. I pulled my wallet out and handed him a twenty dollar bill, "Can I have a pack of antibiotics?"

"Do you have a prescription from a doctor?"

"No, I don't."

"Oh…you need a prescription to buy antibiotics."

"How much will it cost to see a doctor?"

"I don't know…depends which doctor you go to," he scratched his head and said, "it can be somewhere around a couple of hundred dollars."

"I don't have that kind of money."

"Do you have health insurance?"

"No, I don't."

"Then you just have to pay him out of pocket…"

I thanked the pharmacist for his time and brought my swollen nose out without getting any medicine. Two hundred dollars—the equivalent of ten thousand rupees, a decent monthly salary in India—was a bit much to spend on a pimple and an obscene amount of money to be giving away as a consulting fee to a doctor. I could get pimples all my life in India and still not spend that much. The biggest consulting fee I had ever paid to a doctor was two hundred rupees, four dollars. Two hundred dollars was a good chunk of the money that I had brought with me to the United States; I decided to bear the pain and wait until it healed on its own.

A couple of weeks later I got a letter in the mail saying that I needed to get my medical checkup done for my green card application. We scheduled an appointment with a doctor designated by the U.S. immigration services. Charlottesville has several doctors and two big world class hospitals, but we had to go to a small clinic thirty miles away from our home. We drove for thirty minutes and arrived at the clinic—that looked like a small cottage—in the middle of nowhere. The building was surrounded by green mountains and open grassy fields. It looked like a place where one would go to get away from the hustle and bustle of the city and relax in a cozy bed—not lie on a doctor's stretcher. Wondering about the place, we presented ourselves to a middle-aged plump lady wearing a V-necked top with a flowery print. We talked to her through a square hole in the wall in the doctor's lobby.

She asked if we wanted to see Dr. Baynor. Yes, we said, and then she asked us to wait.

The walls in the lobby were covered with very festive-looking wallpaper and some happy music came out of the speakers built into the ceiling. Health and nutrition magazines were strewn across the coffee table and people of different sizes and ages waited patiently. A few minutes later, another lady of alarmingly large size—who could have used some medical attention herself—came out and called my name. She ushered me into the doctor's room. A short-bearded man with a pair of glasses perched on his nose and another pair hanging from his neck came into the room and introduced himself as Dr. Baynor and shook my hand. He sat me down in his room and asked several questions about what I did for a living, where I worked and where I lived, and other introductory matters. I was expecting him to get down to business and tell us what to do for our medical exams. I felt comfortable with his personable nature and I began to like him. Since he didn't seem to be in a hurry and took a lot of interest in our personal lives, I asked him what kind of tests he needed. He answered, "I don't care if you have cancer, heart disease, or kidney disease. You can have as much of those as you want. I just want to make sure you don't have HIV, tuberculosis, or any other disease that you may pass on to people in America." I was taken aback with the doctor's sudden change of disposition. A few minutes ago he sounded like he cared about us more than our own parents.

Before I came to the United States, I had to get several blood tests to prove I was disease free. I told Dr. Baynor that I had gone through a thorough medical check-up less than three months ago and had all the documents to prove it. He said, "Unfortunately, we will have to go through the whole process again."

He took my blood sample and sent me to a different hospital for a chest x-ray. The test results came back negative, but I wondered why the doctor didn't think of my wife as a potential danger to the American people's health; she had been married to me for more than six months and if anyone could get infected because of my illness, Holly would be the first—she would have all the germs that I had. Perhaps it didn't occur to him—or to the US government—that she was equally capable of spreading those diseases.

A couple of months later, I contracted diarrhea. I waited for a couple of days for it to go away but it didn't—it got worse. Now that I had health insurance, my wife decided to take me to the doctor. We arrived at the doctor's office and checked in at the counter. A tired-looking young woman with puffy eyes asked me if I had health insurance even before she asked me what kind of health problem I had. It was like a waitress asking a customer if he brought his wallet with him before she handed him the menu. Since I had health insurance this time, I took out the plastic card and presented it to her in a way that I showed my report card to my mother when I passed a math test after several attempts in middle school. She noted down the details and took us to a different room to wait. Another lady named Betsy—who wore loose green pajamas and a matching top, the kind I wear when I go to bed—appeared with a blood pressure machine, her eyes twinkling. She took my blood pressure and asked me to wait for the doctor. After a short while, a young-looking doctor arrived with a laptop in his hand and introduced himself in a way as we were a long time buddies. He asked us, "What's goin' on, guys?"

I said, "Not so well…is there a restroom close by?"

"Right around the corner to your right…"

A few minutes later, I returned, wiping the sweat off my forehead.

He responded, "Looks like you got diarrhea…"

I said, "I am not sure what it is…I don't recall eating anything bad."

He sat me down and started interrogating me about the diseases my mother, father, grandmother and grandfather had had. He kept typing on his laptop as I answered his questions. The last doctor I had seen didn't care whether I had cancer, kidney disease or a bad liver. This guy not only wanted to know about the diseases I had in past but also made a note of the illnesses my folks had back in India. He asked me if he could get my permission to see the chest x-ray results from my last visit to the doctor. When I told him I didn't have it with me, he said, "Don't worry about it… we can get the hospital to send it to me." I was impressed that the hospital had it stored in its database and was surprised that he had to ask my permission to use it. When the doctor left us alone for a minute, I asked

Holly why he needed my approval. She said, "It's a privacy issue…the hospital can get in trouble if they release your medical records without asking you."

A few years ago, I took Holly to our family doctor in Lucknow to get blood work done. I don't remember what it was for, but it must have been something negligible. Quite a few days passed and we forgot about that visit but one day my father came to me and said, "Congratulations!" Surprised, I said, "What about?" He said, "Dr. Tandon said Holly and you had some test done in his clinic." I looked at him in astonishment. He said, "Am I going to be a grandfather soon?" When I told him we didn't go there for a pregnancy test, he said, "Now, what do I do with these two boxes of sweets that I bought to distribute in the neighborhood?" It made Holly angry that our doctor told my parents about her test. She told me Dr. Tandon would have lost everything he owned if he had done this to us in America. I understood what she meant when the doctor in Charlottesville asked for permission to use my chest x-ray results.

While I was still wondering about how different the medical practice was in two different countries, the doctor came back with another young looking colleague. He resembled Leonardo DiCaprio—who played a doctor, among other things—in the movie *Catch Me If You Can*. One of them said to me, "Looks like this is something that you brought from India…"

I looked at him with a confused face.

"We need to do a couple of tests."

I asked, "What for?"

The two of them looked at each other with their foreheads wrinkled and eyebrows strained. After a brief discussion, one of them said, "Since you have just arrived from India, we need to do a small test to make sure you don't have tuberculosis."

I was surprised to hear him say that. I was sitting in front of two doctors with a problem that was causing me to run to the bathroom every thirty minutes and they were least bothered; instead they wanted to do a test for a disease that I never had and had tested negative for twice in the last four months.

Frustrated, I said, "What makes you think I may have tuberculosis and what about the problem that I am here for?"

"We are not sure you have tuberculosis, but it is a mandatory test that we have to do on anyone who has entered the United States less than six months ago. We will also do a test for diarrhea."

I said, "I have gone through an x-ray exam less than a month ago for TB and tested negative...why do you need another test?"

"We need to do a different kind of test. We will give you a small injection in your forearm and if it swells to the size of a quarter, it will mean that you have tested positive," he said that with a stern face.

I agreed to whatever tests he recommended. He left the room and another lady walked in with a syringe in her hand. She injected some medicine in my left forearm and asked me to come back the next day. I left the doctor's office feeling dejected. After a few hours, my arm started to swell. At first, I could not feel any pain—maybe because it was overwhelmed by the pain in the tummy—but as time passed, the arm started to throb and it surpassed all the other problems.

When I woke up in the morning, my left arm was twice the size of the right arm. I was still sick and spent a lot of time in the bathroom and it didn't help that my swollen arm was in severe pain. I went to the doctor dreading to hear what he would say. He looked at my arm and gave me smile that meant, "I was right."

"Yep, you got it. It's positive," he said.

I tried to explain that as a child I had received immunization injections against various diseases including tuberculosis, but that didn't change his decision. He prescribed a nine-month-long treatment for the disease and gave a three-day dosage for my diarrhea. I left his office with a swollen arm and a runny bum.

Holly and I were once again puzzled that he did not say anything about her being infected by me. If the doctor was so convinced that I had TB, then, Holly—who had been living with me—must have contracted the disease, too. We were both worried that both of us might end up being TB patients. The next day she went to her student health office in the university and showed my prescription to a doctor there and explained the whole situation and asked if she should to do a test for tuberculosis too. The doctor looked at my prescription and copied it on another piece of paper and asked my wife to take the same medicines for nine months. He assumed that Holly would definitely be infected and didn't feel the need to do a test. This was very unsettling for both of us. The first doctor made me go through a test that I didn't ask for and the second doctor didn't want to do a test on my wife when she actually wanted one.

After all these incidents with sickness and hospitals, I decided not go to a doctor for little troubles. I started consulting about my health problems with friends who happened to be doctors. I found it much better, since they gave their personal opinion and suggested remedies by making a diagnosis based on their experience and guesses and not by unnecessary medical tests. Since they helped me in a different setting, in a different role and not in a hospital, they didn't worry about me suing them for wrong advice—they had no pressure. The same people acted very differently when they had their white coats on.

I often thought of Dr. Tandon. He used to make me feel me better for a very small fee and never asked me to go through pointless tests. And one time when he told my father about something he wasn't supposed to, we got to eat delicious sweets for two weeks. It wasn't so bad after all.

Naked

~

My father is hydrophobic. So am I. And so is my
whole family. My father has instilled a deep sense
of fear about drowning in all of his children that makes
us shudder at the thought of even riding in a boat on a
shallow river.

A couple of decades ago, my uncle and my family
decided to go on a pilgrimage. They planned on visiting
Vindhyachal, a Hindu pilgrimage site—situated in the
northern state of Uttar Pradesh—which required us to take
a twelve-hour train ride from my hometown, Lucknow.
After travelling overnight, we arrived at the train station
at four in the morning. The station master told my father
that the holy site of Vindhyachal was only a couple miles
away from there. But what he didn't say was that we had
to cross the Ganges River. My father didn't know this when
we left our home in Lucknow. He got quiet and did not
express any excitement at the fact that we had travelled

the whole night and the destination was only a short boat ride away.

We walked to the river, which was very close to the station. It was a chilly February morning. My uncle asked my dad to look for a boat-wallah. But, my father had something else in mind. I am quite sure he was imagining one of the dreadful scenes from a Bollywood movie where the hero's family is trying to cross a river, but gets caught in a bad storm and everybody ends up losing each other. He suggested that everybody should return home from that point and not visit the shrine. He made the point that it was very chilly and dark and the Ganges appeared very deep and if by any chance the boat sank, we all would die. He reinforced the point by reminding us that none of us knew how to swim. Everyone started to reconsider crossing the Ganges and going to the shrine. My uncle decided that we would take the chance and cross the river; we had travelled for more than three hundred miles to get there, after all.

My father could not argue with him, but that was the last time he rode in a boat. Since my father was always scared of drowning, he advised us not to go anywhere near any body of water more than a foot deep. Although I disagreed with him on various other things in life, I strictly followed this particular piece of advice.

When I came to America, my wife suggested that I should learn to swim. I looked at her and thought, "Are you crazy?" I had no intention of drowning in a pool in America. The Ganges was a much better place to die. She insisted that she would be there to help me learn to swim and that there would be other people who could help me. I still didn't show any interest. It didn't seem like a fun activity to me. I couldn't imagine having fun, revealing my out-of-shape body in public and splashing around helplessly in a massive pool of water. The only time I allow my body to get near more than a bucket of water is when I take a shower. And I don't waste much time in the bathroom, either. I am usually done performing my ablutions in less than ten minutes.

After much coaxing and cajoling, Holly realized that I was not going to make any effort. She got me a membership at the university swimming pool. One day when I returned home from work on a humid August evening, she playfully came up to me and asked, "How are you feeling, honey?"

I said, "Hot and tired!"

She quickly asked again, "How does cool water sound?"

I looked at her, trying to gauge what she was driving at and said, "Sounds good, I guess!"

She grabbed a bag with one hand and my wrist with the other and said, "Let's go swimming!"

By the time I spluttered out a few words—I mean, you know I can't, why don't you understand—she had me sitting in the car and we were driving to the pool. We arrived at the Aquatic and Fitness Center and went inside the building. After walking along a corridor, we arrived at a place where there were two doors facing each other. She pointed a finger at one of them and said, "Go through that door and I will see you in the pool," and went inside the other door. I had never been inside a swimming pool before—I mean never. It didn't make sense to me why my wife would bring me all the way from home to the swimming pool, but would leave me at the door and not take me inside with her. I also wondered why she went through one door and asked me to go through another.

After pondering this for a few minutes, I opened the other door and went inside, hoping I would see a swimming pool. I have to say I still feel disgusted when I remember what I saw inside. There was no swimming pool behind that door. Instead, there was a naked man standing casually with his buttocks facing me. I quickly backtracked and stepped out of the place. I knew the laws in America were strict and I certainly didn't want to get into any kind of trouble by accidently walking into someone's private room. Breathing heavily, I asked a gentleman who happened to pass by in the corridor, "How do I get to the pool?" Pointing at the same door I came out of, he said, "Right through that door."

I wanted to tell him what I saw inside, but he seemed to be in a hurry. I mustered up some courage and opened the door again and walked inside. This time the man who stood with his bare backside facing me, turned around when he noticed me and said, "Hayadoin'?' As he turned towards me he revealed his front and his little guy dangling from his pelvis. I almost vomited at the sight, but he acted as if everything was normal. He didn't even make the slightest effort to hide anything. He had his underwear on his shoulder and a towel in his hands. He appeared to be a man in his early twenties and had a swimmer-like physique.

While he strutted around naked, I stood there in my jeans and shirt, wondering where the pool was. I gave him an apologetic smile—as if it was my fault that he was naked and that it wasn't my idea to come to swim—and looked around to find an entrance to the pool. As he walked away whistling some happy song, another man appeared with a towel that looked like an American flag wrapped around his waist. It looked like he had just taken a shower, since his head was wet with water dripping down his neck and shoulders. He gave me a friendly nod and started watching a football game on a TV mounted on the wall, with his hands crossed in front of his chest and palms tucked under his armpits. I stood there wondering why the first guy was so shameless and naked and appreciated the guy in towel for his decency. I approached him and said, "I am trying to get to the pool."

Without looking at me—and not taking his eyes off the TV—he unfurled his towel and started wiping his head with it, exposing his genitalia. By impulse I took a couple of steps back. I had never seen anyone do that before. The last time I saw something of a similar sort was when someone unfurled a flag with a bunch of flowers wrapped in it, letting the flag wave in the wind and flowers go down. In this case, the flag went up but whatever was wrapped in the towel didn't go down; it just hung in there like a bat holding on to a branch of a tree in deep slumber. It was an amazing sight, and disturbing, too. He was so engaged in watching the game that he didn't hear me. I didn't feel like asking again, and moved away from him.

The next moment, three more naked men appeared from somewhere, all of them wet from head to toe, wiping themselves with towels. The new set of men seemed to know each other, and they discussed politics while they shook their heads to get the water out and casually—not showing any signs of hurry—putting their underwear on. I had never been in a room full of naked men. I felt very self-conscious. I asked one of them to direct me to the swimming pool and he pointed his finger to a door. As I moved towards that door, he stopped me and said, "You might want to change first." It didn't occur to me that I should put on my swimming trunks before I headed for the pool. I pulled a towel out of my bag and wrapped it around my waist tightly, tucking the loose end into the folds, and carefully unbuttoned my jeans and wiggled them off under the towel— making sure no one saw anything—while naked men roamed around me freely.

Having half a dozen totally naked tall and muscular men around made me feel vulnerable in a way that I had never felt before. It reminded me of a scene from a Bollywood film in which the heroine is changing her clothes behind a bush after taking a bath in the lake and all of a sudden four burly guys with bad intentions surround her.

After I put on a pair of knee-length swimming trunks and took my shirt off, I walked through the door to arrive at the pool. I saw my wife standing there waiting for me impatiently. She asked, "What took you so long?" I clenched my teeth—making sure that they were visible through the skin of my jaw—and gave her a look that meant, "I will talk to you when we get home."

She didn't know what was wrong and grabbed my wrist and started walking towards the pool. As I walked with slouched shoulders and head bent down, trying not to see anyone, and trying not to be seen half-naked, I heard a female voice, "Hi, Deepak!" It was Kelly, one of Holly's friends, who emerged from the pool wearing a bikini. She grabbed the step-bars and pulled herself out of the swimming pool. After coming out, she swept her wet hair back with her hands, then perched them on her waist and said, "Good to see you guys!"

It was an awkward moment, as I forced my hands down from wanting to cover my chest while she stood comfortably two feet from me with water seeping through her bikini top, which was pasted to her breasts, showing all the contours. I was freezing more from embarrassment than from cold. I had never been this naked in public and I had certainly never seen this naked a woman in public except in movies. I gestured at Holly to get into the pool—I thought it was better to be in the pool and hide in the water than stand outside and suffer in discomfiture—although I spent all my life avoiding getting into the water.

After we finished talking to Kelly, we descended into the pool. I let Holly step in first and then I slowly made my way into the chilly, highly chlorinated water. I had only spent a few minutes in the facility and my nose was already overwhelmed by the strong stench. I got accustomed to the cold temperature of the water after a few minutes but I still held on to the step-bars and stayed in the corner and at shallowest part of the pool. In the mean time Holly had taken two laps of the pool along with many other fish-like swimmers. Noticing that I was not making much progress she brought some plastic pads and asked me to stick them under my stomach and try to balance on them while holding on to the steel rails. I tried it a couple of times and it worked for a few minutes, but soon the pads would slip out and I would wobble helplessly and frantically try to find my feet on the ground. I continued this process for half an hour and begged Holly to rescue me from this misery and take me home. But, she was not done yet. She told me the best part was still to come. I wondered how horrible the best part was going to be. She promised it would be fun and I didn't have to swim. "Just sit and enjoy," she stressed. I didn't trust her, but agreed anyway.

The next part was sitting in the hot tub—again, something I was not familiar with. She took me to a small circular carved out area in the floor with cemented seats. Hot bubbly water was continuously being ejected into the whole area through small holes all around. Holly wanted us to sit there with some other half-naked people of different ages. She stepped in first. When I put my foot in, the water felt warm. But, as I got deep inside, the water was quite hot and it took some getting used to. I sat there for what felt like an hour and wrestled with gushing hot water which was trying to throw me out of my seat, pushing me from behind.

By the time we finished with the hot tub, I had lost the feeling in my limbs. My legs felt numb and my hands could not even hold a towel. I looked at my wife and asked whether there was anything else she had in mind for that evening or whether she done having fun watching me suffer.

We went home after a short while and I vowed I would never go back to swim.

Striptease

~

After living in the small college town of Charlottesville, I started getting the urge to see a real city. My family and friends back in India had never heard of Charlottesville and they always asked me if I had been to New York, Las Vegas, or Chicago. I thought it was time for me to go visit one of those places. We debated for a few weeks about where to go. One day Holly got an email from her college friend Anna saying that she had moved to Chicago and that we should visit her there; she was living alone in a two-bedroom apartment.

That helped us make up our minds. We decided to go to Chicago. I remembered that my geography teacher in eighth grade made sure all the students in the class knew Chicago's nickname—the Windy City—and that it was built on Lake Michigan. I always remembered it was in the shape of a big tear—one of the biggest lakes in North America. I never got that wrong when I had to fill out cities and lakes in the map of North America on my geography test. I was excited at the opportunity of visiting the city that I had been seeing in an atlas for so many years.

We only had a few days to decide and to plan what to see in Chicago. We were going for four days and there was too much to be seen and covered. We also wanted to make sure to spend enough time with her friend and not end up using her apartment as a hotel. We packed our bags and flew from Charlottesville to Chicago O'Hare International Airport.

When we arrived in Chicago, Anna's mother came to pick us up in her car. After driving for a while, we entered her neighborhood. As we drove some more in that area I started getting a strange feeling; it felt as if I had already been there. But, it didn't make sense, since it was my first time in the Windy city. The place seemed more and more familiar as we approached Anna's apartment—the snow covered streets, brick houses, churches, people dressed in long furry overcoats—all of it seemed very recognizable. While I was still feeling eerie about the whole situation, Anna, who was sitting in the front seat, turned her head behind and said, "Did you know that a lot of American films have been shot in Oak Park?" I took a deep breath and leaned back in my seat—I had found the answer to the puzzle. Just before I left India, I had seen the movie, 'Home Alone,' and it was shot in Oak Park and that's why the place looked so familiar. I was even more excited to be in Chicago; I called my childhood friend in India—I had seen 'Home Alone' with him—to tell him that I was staying in Oak Park. He was excited that I was there and wished that he could be there too. He wanted me to describe everything around Oak Park and also to call him later to tell him if I saw anything else that was exciting or different. I promised him that I would.

After arriving at her place, we rested for a few hours, and in the evening we went downtown for dinner. When we got to downtown Chicago, I have to admit that I turned into a seven-year-old kid who was visiting Disneyland for the first time. Holly and Anna walked ahead of me and they kept losing me as I would slow down or stop to look at the bright lights, tall skyscrapers, people in strange clothes and all the jazz. We walked for a couple miles to eat pizza at one of the Anna's favorite places. I had survived Charlottesville's cold weather and I thought I would easily manage wintertime anywhere in the world. I was wrong. It was the month of March and I had to stop five times—in coffee places, book stores, grocery stores etc.—before we reached the restaurant. I could tell why Chicago was called the Windy City—it was very windy and that made all the difference in the temperature.

We returned home shortly after eating. The next day, Holly and I decided to explore the city on our own. We spent a lot of time in downtown Chicago where among other things I was intrigued by signs that read, Gentlemen's Club, VIP Club, Mr. G's Club, Angie's Pink Club. Every time I saw one such club I paused to read more and asked my wife about it. She always seemed to avoid answering my question by changing the topic. When I insisted, "Please tell me what these places are!" she replied, "You don't want to know," and dragged me by my arm while I kept looking back at the sign.

All of those posters reminded me of R rated movies in India—known as blue films—which are played in rundown theatres. I remember going to see one such movie when I was in high school in India. A group of my friends decided to cut class to go see the movie Blue Lagoon. Hollywood actress Brooke Shields had created a rave among my friends because of her lip-locking scene with Chris Atkins. My parents would have been very upset if they had found out that I went to see that movie. All of us had to make sure no one saw us in or around the movie theatre. We entered after the film had begun, making sure the lights were off and it was dark inside. Following the yellow lights along the aisle we groped our way to the seats. The film had already begun, but we were not worried about missing the plot; we just didn't want to miss the kissing scene. One of us asked the person sitting next to him if we had missed anything 'important', and found out that we made it in time. After watching the film for an hour lights came on for the intermission. I saw someone who looked like my father's friend sitting in the front row. I immediately ducked my head down and pretended I was searching for something that I had accidently dropped between seats. I remember getting up only after the lights were turned off—making sure my father's friend didn't see me.

I couldn't imagine such movies being termed as pornographic in Chicago since I had seen people kissing in the streets and women wearing less clothing in public in America than the ones in those 'adult movies' in India. It seemed impossible for such films to have any market in the city of Chicago.

I got curious and decided to find out about those places. After walking around a while we got hungry and went to eat at a Thai restaurant. After we finished eating, my wife went to use the ladies room. I immediately cornered a waiter and asked him about those clubs. He explained, "Oh, those are strip clubs...people go to see naked women there...there are some good clubs around here."

Surprised, I said, "Really?"

"Yeah, man."

"So, who goes there?"

"Anybody who wants to see naked women..."

While I stood there listening to him with my mouth wide open, he continued with more information. "There are quite a few here...but the one next door is not good," he paused for a minute and then said, "They don't show nothing...but the Gentleman's Club is real good...they got some real good girls there."

I had to finish my conversation abruptly as my wife came out looking for me. It started getting dark and the temperature plummeted. We got on the L—the local train—to go back home. I wanted to talk to someone about those clubs—I needed to get it out of my system. After getting home I called my friend in India again and told him what I saw. He couldn't believe it and asked me to visit one of those places and find out exactly what happens there. I explained that I couldn't go there alone. He insisted that I should go and tell him everything about what I saw. After a lot of persuasion, he got me to promise him that I would go to one of the strip clubs.

It was around 10 p.m. and everyone was lazily lounging and watching TV. Holly was reminiscing about her college life with Anna. I thought about the promise I made to my friend a few minutes ago. I wanted to go to one of the clubs and see what goes on behind the doors in those clubs and then narrate everything to him. But, how was I going to do it? It was getting late and cold and I didn't know the city. Just leaving the house and coming back late at night didn't sound like a good plan. The only way I could make this happen was to take Holly with me. I wasn't sure how she would react. I suggested my idea to her quietly and she raised her eyebrows with an expression that meant, "Just go to sleep!"

I insisted. She brushed me away. I kept nagging without letting Anna know about my plans. Finally, I was able to convince her to come with me. We told Anna that we were going for a stroll outside. It was freezing and streets were lonely. We took the local train at 11:15 pm to go downtown. I noticed a very different crowd on the train since my last ride at 7 pm—passengers dressed professionally had been replaced by people with no destination. It seemed that way because none of them got off at any stops—Austin, Laramie, Cicero, Pulaski, Oakley—and they didn't care where the train was taking them. We didn't know ourselves where we were going, but since we were headed towards the centre of the town, we got off at Ashland.

We took the elevator down and arrived at a narrow street tucked between tall buildings. I had no idea where to find a strip club and there was no one to ask. After walking a few meters, I hailed a yellow cab. We hopped in and I told the driver to take us to the nearest strip club. The Afghani-American cab driver drove us for less than two minutes and parked his car in front of a deserted building and suggested we should open the door and walk right in.

We opened the huge wooden door and peeked inside. I saw a black man sitting behind a counter, dressed in a suit, wearing a pair of headphones and a microphone. He smiled and said, "Come on in!" Without asking what we were looking for, he said, "I need a photo ID from each of you." I nervously showed him my driver's license and Holly did the same. Then he said, "It is twenty dollars per head, but ladies are free." I gave him the money and he asked us to wait for a few minutes. Shortly, a very tall and muscular white man appeared wearing a black suit and headphones and microphone attached to his head. He came to us and shook my hand and said, "Welcome to the Gentleman's Club! Come with me."

He took us a floor above in an elevator. When we got out he asked, "Can I take your jackets?" Not having any experience in a strip club, we didn't know what to say and handed our jackets to him. As soon as he took the jackets, he said, "It is two dollars each to hang them." Again, we couldn't argue with him or even say no. I gave him a twenty dollar bill. I was a little surprised when he returned my change in the form of sixteen ones. I looked at Holly with a question mark on my face and shoved the money in my pocket. We were then led into a massive hall with very dim blue and red lights. The only visible thing was a twenty-foot-long ramp which was illuminated with a high wattage bulb. But, there was no one on the ramp.

Somewhere from the darkness, a young topless lady emerged and said, "How are you guys doing?"

The last time I had seen a topless woman was in an American movie. I blinked a few times when I saw the young lady standing before me with a pair of unclothed breasts and jutting crimson nipples. She was in no rush and asked again, "How are you guys doing?"

I replied to her question, "Fine…"

"Would you like to sit down?"

We nodded and walked behind her, following her glittery underwear which shimmered when it caught a beam of light—it was the only thing we could see in darkness. She sat us down on a semi-circular couch right in front of the ramp and said, "Enjoy!"

As soon as we got settled someone turned on some erotic music with a lady singing like she was getting out of breath. After a few seconds of music a topless woman jumped on the stage and grabbed the pole in the middle of the ramp and started climbing it. She climbed up for about eight feet holding on to the pole with her hands and pushing herself up with her legs. After reaching a certain height she opened up her one leg and an arm and let herself slide down while she supported herself with the other arm and had the other leg wrapped around the pole like a snake.

When she got done with her show another woman with bare breasts performed a similar act. But, she exhibited some more acrobatic skills. She turned her back towards us and spread her legs far apart. And then she bent her torso down with her face showing upside down through the gap of her legs tucked between her breasts. Staying in the same position she made her buttocks jiggle for a few seconds.

Another young woman came dancing and plunked herself down at the edge of the ramp, just a few feet from us. She squatted down and threw both hands back to touch her shoes and made her body look like a bow. Her breasts seemed extra pale and firm like someone had dumped two fresh bowls of yoghurt on her chest; they stayed intact and upright and did not wilt to the side. She stretched her body a little more and brought her head out through the legs, placing it right under her crotch, and blew a kiss at us. No one ever blew a kiss at me, definitely not in that awkward a posture. It was amazing.

My wife looked at me and asked, "Are you having fun?" Realizing that she had been in a bad mood ever since we left Anna's house and that the question was sarcastic, I said, "I can't say I am having fun, but this is definitely something I have never seen before." She replied curtly, "Neither have I."

The show kept going on and the topless women kept walking around giving us strange looks. After all the girls finished dancing, one of them came and sat down next to Holly and started asking us where we were from and what we were up to. It seemed they didn't have a lot of couples as their clients. We were a little self-conscious and I wondered why we were the only people in the club. I asked the girl sitting next to Holly if it usually was so empty. She said, "No honey, you picked the wrong day of the week. No one comes on a Monday night." I didn't realize it was Monday until she told me. It was odd talking to a person wearing only a G-string—my neck-tie probably used more cloth than her dress—and nothing else. The girl was interested in offering us some more services since she kept saying, "Are you guys sure you don't want anything else?" We weren't sure what she meant.

We left after drinking two lemonades and paying four times what they would cost anywhere else. When we came out of the building my wife's anger had reached a new level. She said, "Can't believe you saw naked women?"

I said, "But that's what you did too."

She gave me a mean look and didn't talk to me for the next two days.

Who is Isabel?

~

A few days after I arrived in Charlottesville, we had to call a maintenance man to fix our house's plumbing. The guy looked very different from the plumbers I had seen in India. He drove a huge white pick-up truck which had his company's sign painted across it. He looked very well-fed—compared to the ones in my part of the world who are mostly scrawny and short with cheekbones sticking out and eyes sunken deep in the eyeball socket—and wasn't short of flesh on his body and stood more than six feet tall. He also carried more tools to operate on the choked gutters of the house than some of the Indian doctors I had seen in government hospitals. His pants had several pockets and his waist belt had different sizes of leather bags hanging on to it. He wore a hard hat with a built-in-flashlight and a pair of rubber knee-length boots. He also had a walkie-talkie attached to his right shoulder from which a crackly voice kept talking to him. I had never seen a plumber with so much gear and found it hard to believe that it took so much equipment just to clear a drain of clogged poop. I wanted to see what he was doing so I started a conversation with him. He asked me where I was from. I told him I was from India and had arrived only a week ago. He said, "Just in time for Isabel!"

I could not understand what he was talking about, and thought he was talking about someone important who may be visiting Charlottesville. After the plumber left, I got curious and asked my wife, "Do you know Isabel?"

"No, I don't. Who is she?"

"The plumber told me that I arrived just in time for Isabel."

"Oh, Isabel, the hurricane…!"

"Hurricane!"

"Yep, it's quite a big one. It is headed towards Virginia and it will most likely pass through Charlottesville."

I realized what the plumber meant. I immediately tuned the television to the weather channel and learned that the hurricane was set to arrive in less than a week.

As the days went by and the time for Isabel to arrive got closer, every news channel on the television spewed out warnings and suggestions about what to do in order to be safe. All of Holly's friends talked about Isabel for days. Everyone was worried about how severe it was going to be and what they should do to prepare for it.

I wasn't getting the gravity of the situation. I couldn't imagine it to be a threat. I had witnessed rain and thunder storms in India, but never had to evacuate or watch the warnings—if there were any warnings at all—on TV for weeks. We could never tell when it was going to rain or storm. We just had to run for shelter or stop travelling or doing anything we were doing and let the storm pass and get back on the road after a couple of hours.

On one occasion, it was my cousin's wedding in Lucknow where more than a thousand people were invited. It was a very humid June evening. The reception was supposed to start at eight in the evening, but people started showing up a couple of hours before. It was stifling hot and not a leaf was moving—the air was still. Just when my uncle announced that the food was ready, we heard a rustling sound in the trees. It was a good feeling, since everybody was sweating profusely and a rush of wind made the sweat on our arms and faces feel like a cool shower. Within a few minutes the wind got stronger and started blowing the decorations all over the place. The canopy on the food stalls started to flutter and turn inside out. In the next fifteen minutes, we lost power, and wind combined with heavy rain made people run for shelter. The marriage lawn turned into a big swamp and every single item of food got covered with dirt. The power did not return until the next morning. That was one time we could have used a warning.

In Charlottesville, I could not imagine going through such chaos. The last time I heard about a power outage in America was in 1965 and it became so famous that they made a movie about it—*Where Were You When the Lights Went Out?* I was sure that America—where fire trucks run to help a cat stuck in a tree and police officers surround a small fender-bender with three police cars and an ambulance—should be well-prepared to tackle a hurricane.

A day before Isabel was set to arrive we went to the grocery store to buy some essential items. It seemed like every single resident of Charlottesville was out to shop. There were ten cash registers in the grocery store and all of them had about twenty people waiting to check out. Most of the baskets were filed with almost identical items—rolls of toilet paper, bottled water, milk, orange juice, cereal, bread, etc. I noticed that most of the customers looked worried. We bought some milk and bread and left.

The next day it started raining in the evening. Holly got worried and shut all the windows and doors in the house. She made sure we slept on the first floor and not in our own bedroom, which was on the second floor and could have gotten hit by falling trees. We used our couch, which turned into a bed.

We lay down in the bed and heard the sounds of rain get stronger as every hour passed. The fire trucks bellowed their sirens and every time they paused we heard thunder. Since our house was surrounded by tall trees, I could hear the branches hitting the roof and vines clawing down on the window panes with every gush of the wind. The door creaked and fought hard to stay intact as more than a hundred miles per hour wind hit it with full force. Our house was partially made of brick and partially wood and I felt it being thrashed by wind. At some point in the night we fell asleep.

When we woke up, it was still very dark outside, but the wind had completely stopped. I could not hear anything—birds were not chirping, people weren't walking by, cars weren't passing though our street—it was very quiet and I thought it was still the middle of the night or very early in the morning. I got out of bed and groped in the dark to find the light switch to see the time. I found a switch and turned it on, but it didn't do anything. I tried another one. Nothing happened. The room was still dark. I realized we had lost power. I strained my eyes to see the time on my wrist watch and didn't believe the time. It was eight in the morning, but, it was still very dark outside and there were no signs of life.

I opened the door to take a look. The steps and front yard were covered with wet leaves and broken twigs of different sizes. The rain had stopped, but it clearly had made its impact. I walked out to the street. It seemed like a horror scene out of a movie. No one was out and the cars parked by the side of the road were covered with wet leaves; some of them were damaged by fallen trees. It seemed that most people had fled the city before the hurricane arrived. Their houses had borne the brunt of Isabel's fury. Some of them were missing part of their roofs and some of them had broken windows. Our street was covered with wet trash—loose paper, soda cans, food packages, used tampons—that seemed to have flown out of trash cans. It looked like someone had emptied a giant garbage dumpster from the sky on our street.

The clouds were still dark and threatening to rain again. The house next door had a huge tree fallen on it and the front yard was roped off by a yellow plastic ribbon. I found out that someone had gotten hurt in that house when the tree fell on the chimney and caused it to crack open the roof. I stood around for a few minutes and tried looking for someone I could talk to, but I didn't see anyone. I went back into the house to tell Holly what I saw. She was worried about the situation and told me that we could not have tea because our electric stove couldn't be used.

I am accustomed to having power cuts but it never took a hurricane to knock it off in India. It was an order of the day—load shedding, children getting their kites stuck in the overhead electrical wires or a monkey jumping on the cables—anything could disrupt the power supply. It was never a surprise coming back home after a long day of work to learn that the power had been out for hours.

When Holly told me that we lost power because of the hurricane she meant a bigger problem than I could have imagined. Not having power in that house in Charlottesville meant we couldn't eat because the cooking range was electric powered. We couldn't make a phone call because the phone was cordless and it needed to be charged by electricity. We could not use our computers for the same reason.

In India, when we lost power, we found it hard to go to sleep in the hot and steamy summer nights with mosquitoes feasting on our blood. I would lie in bed—after hopelessly waiting for many hours for the power to come back—and stare at the ceiling fan, desperately wishing for it move. I tried sleeping in different positions, sometimes on my back, on my side and sometimes facedown, in an effort to get comfortable. At some point, usually very early in the morning, totally drenched in my sweat, I would feel a cool breeze blowing down on my face from the ceiling. I would instantly look up to see the fan moving and all the bulbs lit in the house. Everyone would yell in celebration— the light is back!—and quickly get up and turn off all the light bulbs and go back to sleep.

Apart from feeling hot and not being able to sleep, losing power in India never brought such consternation as I experienced in Charlottesville. We did not have power for three entire days. Since we did not have a stove that worked, someone who had a gas stove invited us for dinner a couple of times. We went to her place and had a candlelight dinner with eight other people. She was the only person with a gas stove in that neighborhood.

It was a lot easier being without electricity in India because people took power cuts in their stride and were prepared for such occurrences on a daily basis. People's daily lives were not disrupted if they lost power for a few hours. As kids, we had to study for exams or finish our homework whether we had electricity or not. If I ever told my teacher that I couldn't finish my homework because there was a power cut in my area, I would get laughed at by the whole class—the teacher would ask me to come up with a better excuse. Often times, I had to study by a candle or lantern's light. Later, we got battery-operated emergency lights.

We spent two nights illuminating our house with candles in Charlottesville; it reminded me of home. The only difference was that we couldn't keep ourselves warm since the heating didn't work and we didn't have thick quilts. In India, we never had central heating, but always had a huge metal box full of quilts.

I had never imagined I would travel ten thousand miles to come to America to experience this.

The Correct Side

~

I never owned a car in India. Since I didn't have one, I never bothered to learn to drive. When I turned sixteen years old, I started nagging my father to get me a motorcycle. He didn't think it was a good idea and worried that I could easily get into an accident. Even when I rode my bicycle around town, he would often tell me to be careful, not go too fast, and always watch out for bigger vehicles on the road. After coaxing for many years—and all my friends taunting me that I still rode a bicycle—he bought me a scooter when I finished my master's degree. By that time, I didn't know anyone in my college who didn't have a motorbike. When my friends decided to go somewhere, they took me with them or I rode my bicycle. I was very pleased to get my first scooter, and I used it for all kinds of purposes—go to work, take my father to his doctor's appointments, grocery shopping—and of course, to drive Holly around for fun; she loved riding on it. I didn't quite understand why she liked it so much, because my scooter—a Bajaj model—was the kind of vehicle which was mostly driven by middle-aged pot-bellied half-bald men who carried their whole family on it—a kid standing on the footrest in front and the wife sitting sidesaddle, holding another kid in her arms. A good way to turn off a girl on your first date was to show up on my scooter—it had zero sex appeal. My father had done his research before he bought me that machine; he had asked his friends who were in their early to late fifties. He thought it was safe, sturdy, economical, and had lots of room for carrying groceries.

I don't know whether I was a good driver or whether the scooter was too slow, but I only had two accidents in my driving years in India. They both involved animals—a dog and a donkey. It was my fault on both occasions since stray animals in India generally have good traffic sense. They are used to dealing with hundreds of vehicles on the road. I often noticed that a dog at a hundred feet looks in both directions before crossing a busy street. It often tries to judge the speed of the oncoming vehicle and then decides whether it should wait or run. I have never seen a dog crossing a street leisurely.

In my case, I was riding my scooter and I saw a dog at a distance of twenty feet. It looked at me and lunged forward in a motion that suggested that it wanted to cross the street. I couldn't react fast enough and kept going at the same speed—I should have slowed down. The dog was clever enough to see that I didn't slow down. It had better control of its reflexes than I had over my scooter—it stopped in its tracks. I got confused and I slowed down too but, the dog wasn't intelligent enough to know how stupid a driver I was. In this game of speeding and slowing down, the distance of twenty feet was reduced to a foot and the next thing I knew my scooter slipped on a banana skin and I fell down. The dog happily crossed the street while I lay on the street helplessly and my scooter's engine was still running and the wheel spinning in the air.

The other incident was when I was riding a motor bike with my wife. I was driving slowly, since the visibility was low due to dense fog combined with dust and pollution. The headlights of oncoming vehicles were only visible when they came within less than twenty feet. The only way to tell whether something was a motorbike or a car was by looking at the dimly lit headlights. But sometimes it was hard, since the three wheeler auto rickshaws had only one headlight, but were just as wide as some of the cars. I was driving with my eyes strained to focus on those vehicles and wasn't looking out for other things. Somewhere along the way, I felt my knuckles brushing against rough skin. I immediately put my foot down on the brakes but it was too late. The handlebar of my motorbike turned in a direction that I didn't want to go and then I felt my entire right arm graze against a bony structure covered with hairy skin. After losing my balance and being pushed onto the unpaved road I realized that I had hit a donkey. I could have avoided hitting him had my wife not been riding with me. Her body weight was thrust on me and made it hard for me to stop sooner—she didn't expect me to stop suddenly. I got squished between her and the donkey.

I had never imagined that I would ever encounter such a tableau—Holly, me, and the donkey. While I was shaken up by the collision and disgusted by the donkey odor on my body, the animal didn't move—it stood there in the same position as when I hit it. We got back on my bike and on the road again. After I got home I took a long shower and checked for any fleas that may have leapt onto me from the donkey.

Apart from the above two accidents I can't recall any other mishaps in my driving years in India. After I came to America, I got the opportunity to learn to drive a car. My wife owned an American car. The vehicle—an Oldsmobile sedan, solidly built, red with a hint of purple color—was given to her by her grandparents and was not a small car by any means. I had never seen so large a car in India; it was quite big even by American standards. Initially, I tried my hand at it by backing out of the driveway and in the process I crushed the plants and the fence in the front yard. I asked my wife if she could teach me to drive, but she suggested I should go to a driving school.

I liked her suggestion and looked in the phonebook and found a teacher. She gave me two options: One, I would have to drive my own car to get to her school. Two, she would pick me up and drop me off at my house after the lesson was over. I went with the latter and more expensive option, since it was difficult for me to get to her and then come back. The teacher was a middle-aged lady with long white hair. The first day she picked me up and took me to her school. She walked with me to an old-looking bashed up car and asked me get in the driver's seat. I got in the car and waited for her to join me. Standing two feet away from the car, she said, "I want you to get familiar with the car first. Turn on the headlights." I looked on the dashboard and found the knob for the headlights. "Now turn on the turn signal," she commanded. I obeyed.

"Check the brake lights."

I put my foot on the brake and a small red light came on the dashboard indicating the brake lights worked.

"Now, get out of the car," she told me.

As I opened the door and started coming out, the car started making a beeping sound.

"Get back in…the car is talkin' to ya!" She screamed at me.

I pulled my leg inside the car and shut the door.

She said, "You forgot to turn the headlights off."

I turned the lights off and came out.

She said, "You don't wanna leave your car if it's beepin' atcha, alright?"

I swallowed nervously and nodded in agreement. She asked me to follow her to a circular track with a diameter of no more than twenty feet and a small grassy island in the middle. She pointed towards another old car with paint peeling off its body and asked me get in the driver's seat.

She told me to drive in a circle without touching the edges of the track. I drove around for a few times, occasionally encroaching on the edge of the circle and sometimes barely missing it. After an hour of lesson she took me home. My wife asked me, "How was the lesson?" I told her that the last time a teacher scared me so much was in the fourth grade.

A couple of days later it was time for my next lesson. The teacher told me that she was going to have me drive on small roads in Charlottesville. I said to her, "I am not sure that I can do that." She replied, "Yes, you can." She seemed more confident about my driving skills than I was. I had never driven a car before and taking a car out on an American road seemed like a huge challenge to me. If I was learning to drive a car in India, I would just be learning to drive. In America, I was learning how to drive a car and at the same time I had to learn to drive with a new set of traffic rules—following the speed limit, obeying the unsaid rule of first come first go at stop signs, stopping for pedestrians, and a hundred other new regulations. I wasn't sure if my teacher was aware of all this.

She put me in a new-looking sedan and asked me to pull out of the parking lot and get on the road. I took the car out of the parking lot and in an effort to get on the road, I started going towards the left side of the road. I suddenly felt my car was going in a direction I didn't expect it to go. I looked to my right and realized my teacher was holding on to my steering wheel with her left hand aggressively and pulling it towards her. When I got on to the right side of the road, she looked at me and yelled,

"WHAT DO YOU THINK YOU WERE DOIN'? WHY WERE YOU TRYNNA DRIVE ON THE WRONG SIDE OF THE ROAD...WHY?"

The only person who yelled at me like this was my mother and I can't even remember the last time that happened. Taken aback by her shouting, I meekly tried to explain that I had recently arrived from India and people drive on the other side of the road there.

She lowered her voice and said, "Okay, okay," and stressed the words, "this is the United States of America and this is not how we do it here...you gettin' my point?" I didn't feel like explaining that I already knew that people drive on the right side of the road in America and that I couldn't unlearn my Indian habit in one day. I was getting frustrated by her constant yelling and treating me like a kindergarten kid.

On my third lesson, I made it a point to tell her how much I appreciated her lessons, but hated her yelling. She said, "Why didn't you tell me earlier? You know, I can get in trouble for that." I told her I could be a better student if she treated me a little bit more nicely. Sitting next to me in the car, she said, "You know it is hard...because I do this for a living and I do this every day...and I can't stand to see people make stupid mistakes...but I will try to be nice to you." I had been driving for more than an hour and I asked her if we could finish our lesson for the day. She said, "Looks like the blood is going to your butt instead of your brain...I know you are tired but I am gonna push, keep drivin.'"

For most of the lessons she had me drive at the speeds between 35 and 45 miles per hour. But one day when I was almost done and very tired after driving for more than an hour, she told me, "Take that exit." I slowed down and turned right to get on the ramp. While I wondered where she wanted me to go, since we had never been on that route before, I heard her say, "Hit the gas!" I was driving at 35 miles an hour at the time. I pressed my foot down on the gas pedal—causing the car to move at 45 miles per hour. The exit ramp was no longer than 300 meters.

I heard her say again, "HIT THE GAS!" much louder than the last time. As I nervously pressed on the accelerator, she said, "WE GONNA DO 65." I couldn't believe her, since she did not tell me at the beginning of the lesson that we would be driving on the highway and that I would have to drive at 65 miles an hour. As I approached the highway and saw vehicles flying at high speeds, I gave her an inquisitive look meaning, "Are you serious?" Before I could say anything, she screamed again, "65, RIGHT NOW!"—as if I was not driving a car but flying a plane and I had to takeoff before I ran out of runway.

I hit the gas full throttle and remembered the lord and thought this could well be my last day. The car was flying—at least that's how it seemed to me—and I tightened my grip on the steering wheel. As I drifted from one lane to the other, she asked me to stay in my lane and be calm. At 65 miles an hour, I couldn't tell whether I was driving the car or the car was driving me. The grip of my fingers on the steering wheel got tighter every time I saw the needle go up on the speedometer—50, 55, 60, 65 miles per hour—as if holding on to the steering wheel could save my life should I crash the car. The only thing that I could hear through the loud combustion of the car engine was my pounding heartbeat.

The highway didn't seem like it had an end—it kept going—and I wondered if I would ever get to stop. After a few minutes, I saw an intersection with traffic lights. I could see the green lights from about half a mile away. It stayed green until I approached it and as I got closer—still driving at 65 miles an hour—it turned yellow. My mind had gotten used to taking orders from the teacher and had lost the ability to use my own common sense. I looked at the lights and asked her, "Should I stop?" She said, "It's your call." I kept going as I was already under the lights by now. Suddenly, my car took a full circle spin in the middle of the intersection and came to a screeching halt. I have never been on a roller coaster ride, but I am sure it must be similar to what I experienced. The papers and decorations on the dashboard were thrashed around and the notepad in the teacher's lap hit my face, causing my eye glasses to slide down from my nose to my mouth, hanging from one ear. I did not apply the brakes and did not understand why the car came to a sudden stop. When the car stopped after making a squealing noise and an impression of its tires on the road, the teacher yelled, "GOD BLESS AMERICA!" I fixed the glasses on my face and looked at her. She said, "When it turns yellow, you don't speed. You stop, okay!"

I said, "Okay." I found out that she had another set of brakes under her seat, which she had used to stop the car. I was already very tired and this treatment was the last thing I needed. I couldn't wait for the lesson to get over. We took the next exit and got off the highway.

The teacher calmed down towards the end of the driving classes and after two weeks of yelling, braking, yanking at the steering wheel and being harsh, I realized that she had actually taught me some useful things—don't park between two cars if there are other spots available, don't cross your arms when turning the steering wheel, look behind your shoulder and don't just rely on the rearview mirror when changing lanes, that sort of thing. Soon after my driving classes ended, I passed the driving test and got my driver's license. I had never worked so hard to take any other test before.

Volunteer

~

Holly suggested that I should work as a volunteer in some organization while I was waiting for my work permit. She thought it would be a good idea to get my foot in the door and also to see what it is like to work in an American setting. I didn't know anyone who had volunteered to work for no money in an organization and I didn't know any company in India that accepted volunteers.

Although there is no formal set up for volunteer work in India, I had seen people volunteer in times of need. My friends, relatives, and neighbors always came to help when my family needed assistance and I was expected to do the same if they needed me. People were always willing to do anything—offer their cars to use as an ambulance if there was an emergency, money, physical presence, to cook food, to watch kids, to offer emotional support and everything else.

Once when my family had to come up with a big sum of money to pay my graduate school fees at short notice, we didn't feel comfortable asking anybody for help. Our neighbor and a long-time friend showed up at our door unannounced one day and noticed our worried faces. When we shared our problem with her, she volunteered to help us out by lending us the required sum. I was able to pay the fees on time and my father returned her money in a few weeks. This could have been arranged by borrowing money from a bank, but that would have required a lot of running around and much paper work—we didn't have enough time. The lady who helped us out is quite elderly now and her children have moved away, but my parents, who still live in the same city as her, try to help her with doctor's visits, money or visiting when she is lonely.

It was quite common for people—mostly older people—in my neighborhood to summon me or my friends to run errands for them. Once I was playing cricket on the street and a friend of my mother called my nickname from the balcony of her third story apartment, "Deepu!" I paused for a moment in the middle of bowling a crucial ball in a decisive game and looked up to see who called; I saw a cloth bag flying down at me. "Go get two kilos of potatoes and a kilo of tomatoes…and make sure they are not rotten…last time you picked out all the bad ones," my mother's friend commanded, "grab that bag!" I hated having to stop my game to get her vegetables, but there was no way out. I couldn't say no to her, because my mother would be upset with me if she found out that I disobeyed her friend's small request. I would have to listen to her telling me for days how nice Mohit was—some guy in the neighborhood—he never refused anybody's requests and that I had earned a bad name by not getting potatoes for her friend. Like most of my other friends, I was conditioned to listen to my elders, even if we didn't agree with them.

Working in an organization as an unpaid assistant was a new concept for me, although it seemed like a good idea that companies invited people to work as volunteers—it gave people an opportunity to gain work experience and companies got a chance to test their future employees.

I took my wife's advice and started looking for volunteer work in the job advertisement section of various newspapers. Since I had enough experience obeying and taking care of my elders, a volunteer opportunity in a retirement home caught my eye. I dressed up and hopped on a city bus to visit the place. I presented myself at the given address and was greeted by a representative. A middle-aged lady dressed in a red knee-high skirt and a jacket handed me a few pamphlets and said, "Take a minute to read these and I will be right back." I glanced through the reading material and waited for her to come back. After a few minutes she returned and said, "So, what do you think?"

"Yes, I would like to volunteer here."

"Why do you want to volunteer?"

I told her I was waiting for my work permit and I wanted to utilize my time.

"Okay, what do you think you can help us with?"

I asked, "What would you like me to help you with?"

"You can help us in a lot of different ways...serve food to the residents, take care of the garden, entertain, paperwork, and most of all the elderly residents need company...they get lonely."

"I would be willing to do whatever I can."

"Oh, you guys make me look so good."

"What do you mean?"

"I am the volunteer coordinator and my job is to find volunteers. So, people like you who want to work here, make my job easy."

I smiled and said, "So when can I start?"

"Tomorrow, if that works for you?"

"Sure."

After we settled on working three days a week from 10 am to 1 pm, she gave me a tour of the building and introduced me to other staff members and to some of the residents.

I came back the next day, ready for my first day of work in the new country. A tall bearded gentleman, Bill, greeted me and swiped his ID card to open a door that led to a spacious hall; the high ceiling and tall windows illuminated the area. The floor was carpeted and wooden chairs lined every wall in the hall. Bill, who was a staff musician, introduced me to a group of residents—some of them sitting on chairs and some in wheelchairs. Some of them looked at me and smiled, and some raised their hands to say hello. Bill showed me a place to hang my jacket. He told me, "You should just watch how the place works on your first day."

After spending a day in the retirement center, I was impressed with the facilities they provided to the residents— good quality food, a garden, good living conditions and even an in-house musician for entertainment. I sat next to Rob, a seventy-eight-year-old man, and asked him about his life. He said his son had left him there because he was too much of a burden for him. Rob was paralyzed, and he couldn't walk. I asked him if he liked being in the retirement home. He said, "It's okay...they take good care of me...I like Bill...he is a good guy." I found it hard to understand him, since the paralysis had impaired his speech, but he wanted to talk to me and I could tell that in the professionally scrubbed atmosphere of that retirement home, he missed human touch. He wanted someone to sit next to him and talk and listen to his stories. In the forty minutes I spent with him, he asked me several times, "Are you gonna come tomorrow?"

There was Sylvia, an old black lady with short white hair. She was sitting alone. I said hello to her, and she held my hand and pulled me down to sit next to her. She asked me, "Where you from?"

"India," I said.

"Can you sing?"

I didn't understand why she asked that but I said, "I can't sing, but I can play harmonica."

"Oh, you do?"

"Yes, I do."

"Go ahead and play then."

I told her I didn't have my harmonica with me that day and promised to bring it with me the next day. When she saw me the next day she immediately asked, "Are you gonna play some music for us today?" I said yes and asked Bill if I could play some Indian tunes for everyone. He enthusiastically announced to everybody that they were going to listen to a different musician that day, "Deepak is going to play his harmonica today and give me a break." He asked everyone to sit in a circle, and placed a chair in front of them for me to sit and play my music. I was nervous, as I hadn't played in years and I wasn't sure if they were going to like Bollywood music. I played a song and was surprised by the response; at first they kept quiet, but thirty seconds into the song everyone started slapping their thighs and tapping their feet and singing along some song that I didn't know. Bill told me the tune of the Hindi song I played was close to a 1960's popular American song. I played a couple of more songs on demand and everyone seemed to enjoy it.

About two decades ago my uncle had bought me a harmonica which happened to become my childhood hobby; I had never imagined that I would entertain people in America with an instrument that I had learned to play as a kid.

I enjoyed working in the retirement home and spending time with the residents, but it made me sad listening to their stories and watching them sit alone and stare at the walls.

They were provided with everything in that place, except a person who could be their friend and companion. The people who worked there were nice and very courteous, but it was their job to be nice to the residents; almost like the air hostesses in a plane who are there to make your journey comfortable, but won't sit down and talk to you.

Often times, on my way back home from the retirement center, I would look out the window of the city bus and see people playing with their dogs on the perfect looking lawns in front of beautiful and spacious homes in Charlottesville. I wondered how they were so nice to their dogs, but didn't have room for the elderly folks. They showed so much love and care for their pets, but wouldn't hesitate to send their parents to a retirement home. It made me very sad; it made me miss my parents.

While I continued working at the retirement home, another volunteer opportunity came up at a local public radio station. Since I had spent two years producing radio shows for the BBC in India, and that is what I wanted to continue doing in the States, I wrote to the news director asking for an interview. The station was looking for announcers. The news director wrote back promptly and asked me to meet him at the station with three pieces of local news. I was excited at the opportunity and started doing the research for the stories.

I looked up the address on the internet and it didn't seem too far—I decided to walk. I arrived at the place looking for a big obvious-looking radio station. But, according to the address, the building number turned out to be an apartment in a small residential building. I knocked on the door hesitatingly. A middle aged man wearing shorts and a wrinkled T-shirt with tousled hair and a stubble opened the door and said, "Deepak?"

I said, "Yes."

"Come on in," he said, "I am Mike. Nice to meet you"

"Nice to meet you, too…"

"Make yourself comfortable…I will be right back."

The lobby of the studio looked like it had been burgled and the thieves had tossed things around and taken everything with them, except the trash. A dirty couch lay in one corner with cigarette holes and dog hair and wet spots. The other corner had a desk with a dust-covered desktop computer which had a crate of bottled water sitting on top of it. The floor had loose paper strewn all over. I looked for a place to sit down and found a tiny revolving chair with no arm rest; as I tried sitting on the wobbly seat, one of the wheels came loose and rolled off to the other end of the room. I gave up on the idea of sitting. The place looked more like someone's home than a professional public radio station. I was expecting it to be organized with the latest technology and a nice lobby with comfortable seating.

I could hear the music in the room and I noticed a lady with a pair of headphones standing in front of a microphone attached to the ceiling—she was visible through a glass hole in the upper half of the studio door. Her lips matched the sound coming out of the speaker in the room.

After a few minutes, Mike came out and asked me to come inside the studio. He said, "You have your stories with you?"

"Yes," I said.

"I want you to read your news at the top of the hour."

"You mean, live?"

"Yes, can you do it? You don't have to if you don't want to."

I was a little taken aback. I wasn't prepared to go live on air and wasn't sure about having my voice heard by thousands of people in Virginia; Mike hadn't told me about this before.

I thought about it for a minute and said, "I will do it."

I read the news. After I finished Mike asked me to step out of the studio. I saw him and the lady talking. A few minutes later he came out and said, "We are having issues with your accent. Can you pronounce words like Bag-Dad and Pack-Is-Tan correctly? You seemed to say Bughdaad and Paakistaan."

I knew I didn't sound American and I had an Indian accent, but I was surprised to hear him complain about the two words that I had actually pronounced correctly.

I said, "But that is the correct pronunciation."

"It may be correct, but our listeners won't understand… they are used to hearing Pack-is-tan and Bag-dad."

"So, you want me to pronounce them incorrectly?"

"I don't know what's correct but people will definitely not understand it the way you pronounced it," Mike said,

"I am willing to give you another chance if you want to try again."

I agreed and I read the news one more time, trying to say the names 'correctly'. I tried hard to sound like Mike but I couldn't do it because I knew that was not proper.

The news director had another two-minute meeting with the lady inside the studio and came out biting his lower lip with his teeth. Without looking in my eyes he said, "I am sorry but I won't be able to offer you this position at this time...we are still having issues with the pronunciation."

I thanked him for letting me try again and left the place, feeling disappointed. I couldn't believe that I was rejected for doing something correctly. It was like an American getting rejected in a foreign country for not being able to pronounce New York correctly.

I was sad that I had lost my chance of working in an American radio station. After hearing what happened to me, one of Holly's friends told me that there was another radio station in Charlottesville and that I should try my luck there. I called and found out that they were looking for news writers. I was happy to know that I didn't have to say names incorrectly, but feared that they might reject me for writing 'wrong' spellings—colour instead of color, defence instead of defense.

Luckily, I got the job as the volunteer news writer and the spell check in the computer fixed my spelling every time I wrote the words correctly.

Sandwiched

~

After a couple of months of working for no money, I started getting flustered—I needed cash, since the money I brought from India started to disappear. I avoided spending money on clothes or shoes. But I soon reached a point where I had to think twice before buying even a small cup of coffee. It felt strange, since I had just quit a cushy job in India and I had gotten used to spending money. Buying a cup of *chai* or a movie ticket—even when I was a student and didn't have a job—had never been a problem. I never thought twice before spending money on my friends; paying for a group of people having *chai* or *samosas* was the order of the day. In less than three months my financial condition had become dire. One time in Charlottesville, a destitute looking guy came up to me and asked, "Can you spare 50 cents for coffee?" I always gave away spare change in India, but that day I realized that I didn't have any money to give away and I could use 50 cents myself.

As the days passed, I kept getting more and more desperate about my work permit. Every day, I would walk to the driveway of our house and check the blue mailbox that was perched on a half-rotten piece of wooden post, tilting downward. It would always have a lot of mail in it; Keith and Liz seemed to be very popular people as every other envelope would have their names on it. I would quickly sift through all of them using my thumb and index finger, but never see an envelope with my name. Disappointed, I would start waiting for the mailman to come the next day and hope that he would bring me good news. I wondered if the mailman thought it was odd that I was the only person who would wait for him. When I asked whether he had anything for me, he would say, "No news is good news." But, one day he said, "You must get off work early to come and wait for me." I told him I was waiting for my work authorization papers and I couldn't work until I had them. He said in a sympathetic tone, "Ah! That explains your anxiety…well…I'll bring it as soon as they send it." Seeing him on a regular basis helped us get closer to each other, and I would sometimes walk to his white postal van—it didn't have any doors and reminded me of auto rickshaws in India—instead of waiting for him to come to the house. He would sort out our mail in the van and hand it to me instead of dropping it in the mailbox. Sometimes, he would just drive by without stopping and say, "Ain't got nothing for ya."

One day, after waiting for weeks, I looked through the letters in the mailbox and I saw an envelope which said in the top left corner, 'US Immigration Services'. My heart started racing and I frantically looked for my name on it. I saw my name through a rectangular window in the envelope. I ran inside the house to show it to Holly. I didn't want to open it myself because I was worried it might not be what I was looking for; I asked Holly to check and see what was in it. She looked at me and smiled and took a deep breath as if to say, "Your wait seems to be over." She sliced the envelope open with a knife and pulled out a paper which had a credit-sized, cream-colored card pasted on it. It had my picture on the right side and 'Employment Authorization Document' written on the top—it was my long awaited work permit. I looked at it and held it in my hands and realized that now I would be able to apply for work and tell the employer proudly that I was legally allowed to work in the United States of America. I wanted to go out and start applying for jobs that very minute. I felt like a kid who goes out to buy cigarettes the day he turns eighteen. Later in the day, I called my parents and gave them the good news.

Now it was time to find a job. I looked for jobs in local public radio stations, but it turned out that most of these places ran on volunteers and not paid staff. People who wanted to volunteer made it hard for people who wanted to do the same job and get paid. It had been a few months since I had worked; I was desperate to get any job in order to bring some money home. Holly had been supporting us with her monthly stipend as a doctoral student, which left us only a couple of hundred dollars to buy food and gas after paying the rent. It didn't help that we had to spend hundreds of dollars for medical checkups, visa, and work permit fees so that I could be a legal alien in the United States.

I started filling out application forms everywhere— TV stations, electronic goods stores, jewelry stores, computer stores, motels, bookstores, newspapers, furniture stores— but no one seemed to look at my application; I didn't get any calls from anywhere. I didn't know what I was doing wrong. Most of these jobs required only a high school diploma and I had a masters' degree in business, an MBA. When filling out the application forms, I used up every single line to describe my education and work experience in India; but it seemed that employers didn't care.

I got frustrated and started calling companies, asking for an interview. After much pestering, I managed to get one interview at a furniture retail store. The lady in her early thirties who wore a pearl necklace and a black dress sat me down on one of the display couches. She quickly glanced at my CV on her clipboard and asked me if I had any experience in retail in the United States. When I told her I didn't have any retail experience at all, she looked at me as if to say, "Why are you wasting my time?" She asked me how I would handle an angry customer. I had never dealt with a customer, let alone an angry one. And then she asked me, "Do you know the difference between a recliner sectional sofa and a sectional sofa?"

I had no idea what she was talking about and looked at her with a blank face. She explained, "The one you are sitting on is a sectional sofa." I looked and saw that it was a long L-shaped sofa. "Alright, Deepak, I have a few more candidates to interview. I will get back to you soon," she said with a forced smile and shook my hand. I could tell right there that she wouldn't call me and if she did, it would be to tell me that I didn't get the job. I left the store feeling disheartened.

One day when I was walking around one of the shopping centers of Charlottesville, I noticed a sign—HIRING!—on the door of a Subway restaurant. I had gotten so distraught that I was ready to work anywhere. I walked in and asked for an application. The owner of the Subway turned out to be an Indian. He introduced himself as Patel and gave me the application form and told me to fill it out right away. I sat down in his store and started writing. He came and sat next to me and stared at me as I filled out the form. Patel asked me, "How long have you been in the United States?"

"Three months."

Have you worked anywhere else before this?"

"No...is that a problem?"

He cleared the corner of his lips with his thumb and index finger and looked out of the glass window and then made eye contact with me.

"Not really...but most Indians are not very comfortable...you know, washing dishes, mopping the floor, and sometimes cleaning the toilet...but this is America...you know...we have to do everything ourselves."

While Patel mentioned this and explained the duties of the

job, I remembered my friends joking in India about me not being able to find a decent job in America and ending up washing dishes in a restaurant. I had told them that I was confident in my qualifications and education and would try my best not to work as a waiter or a dishwasher or to do any other menial job. But here I was, sitting at a table covered with breadcrumbs and looking into the eyes of Mr. Patel, who reeked of onions and garlic, and listening to him describe the job that I was going to have to take.

"We will train you to bake and cut bread, roast meat, and prepare sandwiches...we will start with $6 an hour and then go from there—"

I looked at him blankly.

"If you want the job, come at 12 pm tomorrow." I shook his hand and thanked him.

I came back home and told Holly that I had been offered a job at a sandwich place. She looked at me with sad eyes, knowing that this was the last thing I wanted to do, but she didn't say anything. We both knew we needed the money. It wasn't about the choice anymore. I didn't have any option but to accept the offer.

I showed up at the restaurant the next day at 12 pm. Patel gave me a smile and took me into the staff room—a small cubicle in the back stuffed with a chair and a table and a coat rack.

"You need to wear this shirt," he pulled out a shirt from a bag which had the company's name embroidered on the upper right hand side; it was three times bigger than my size—so that an employee of any size could wear it—and it looked like it had been worn many times before and hadn't been washed recently. Since it was smelly and moist, I asked Patel if I could wear it over my shirt. I didn't want it to touch my skin.

"That's fine," he said, and handed me an equally dirty hat with the company's name on it. Since I was getting trained the first day, he gave me a tour of the restaurant. The front counter had about fifteen square steel containers built into it. They were filled with different kinds of meats and vegetables—turkey, beef, bacon, lettuce, tomatoes, onions, peppers, and all the other fixings for sandwiches. There was an oven in the kitchen which baked different kinds of breads. Patel told me I shouldn't worry about making sandwiches on my first day, but, instead, pay attention to what customers ask for. I couldn't imagine it being too hard since I could speak and understand English. A few minutes into my first day of work, a customer walked into the store.

Patel promptly moved towards him and whispered to me, "Listen to him."

The customer said, "Can I get a Turkey on six-inch?"

Patel slid his hands into a pair of plastic gloves and asked, "Wheat or white?"

"White, please!"

Patel pulled out a loaf of bread and cut it into half and laid three round slices of meat on it.

"What kind of cheese?"

"Swiss, please!"

The owner spread the cheese on the bread and slid the bread on to his right, towards the salad on the counter, "What do you want on it?"

"Banana peppers, olives, jalapeño, and some mayo."

Patel added everything he requested and within seconds he wrapped up the sandwich and asked, "For here or to go?"

"To go…"

"Is that it?"

"That will do it."

After listening to half a dozen customers I learned the various ways people asked for things, for example, 'turkey on 6 inch' meant turkey sandwich on 6-inch bread and the question 'for here or to go?' implied to eat here or to take it with you. In the beginning it all seemed too out of context. I remembered ordering a sandwich in my favorite restaurant in Lucknow and saying, "Sandwich 34,"—meaning three sandwiches for four people. It was a common way of ordering but was quite confusing for people who weren't familiar with it. The second day I learned to cut the bread, which seemed like quite an art. At least that's how Patel put it. He called himself a sandwich artist.

"If you want to be a sandwich artist, you have to cut the bread in such way that…" he slid his tiny knife around the bread delicately and cut it open from the three sides and said, "…all the stuffing should stay inside the sandwich and the bread intact." I started making sandwiches but Patel wasn't always happy with my preparation and he would take me in the back and say, "You are giving too much lettuce in the sandwich…you know that's expensive and raises the cost for us."

After giving me a lesson in sandwich-making he said, "Let's show you how to do the cleaning." He brought out a bucket full of dirty-looking water and a mop which was a long plastic stick with a big piece of rag attached to it. He soaked the rag in the water and started mopping the floor, dragging little pieces of bread, lettuce, and onions with it. He dipped the rag into the bucket again, wrung the filth out, and started again. While I was watching him, he suddenly thrust the mop into my hands and walked away. I couldn't understand why he did that. A few seconds later, an Indian family walked into the store and greeted Patel. Still confused, I continued mopping. The whole time the family—apparently his friends—stayed in the store, Patel didn't come anywhere near the bucket of water or the mopping stick. Instead, he acted very much like an owner, pointing at his workers, asking them to do this and that. After his friends left, he grabbed the mop out of my hands and started cleaning again. Throughout the day, I noticed Patel stop cleaning as soon as any of his acquaintances walked in the store. I remembered him mentioning to me about Indians being uncomfortable with doing menial jobs, but I could tell even after living in America for years he himself was conscious of his image among his friends and family.

Towards the end of the day, a tall white boy walked in. He held the buckle of his belt—to stop his pants from falling down—with one hand and a cell phone in the other.

His pants were already down to his knees and caused him to walk in a funny way; he dragged his legs. He approached the counter, still talking on his phone, bringing it closer to his mouth when he spoke into it and then putting it back to his ears when he listened—he pretended as if it was a walkie-talkie. Looking in my eyes, he said, "Umm…y'all sold a sandwich to my girlfriend yesterday…umm…she didn't want tomatoes on it…umm…and y'all put tomatoes on it…she is sick now."

I didn't know what to say to him and couldn't tell what he wanted us to do for him. Pay for his girlfriend's medicine? Give him the money back for the sandwich? Apologize and make him a new sandwich? I had no idea. Patel heard the guy complain from the back room, he quickly came out and said, "Sir, we make everything in front of you and ask you what you want on it…I can't imagine putting tomatoes on the sub when she didn't ask for them."

The guy didn't say anything, just kept looking at us. After a brief pause, he left the store. Patel turned to me and said, "You will have this every now and then…he just wanted a free sandwich…I understand…he was hungry. If he had asked me for a free sandwich without accusing us…I would have happily given it to him…you know."

Just before leaving for the day, Patel told me, "I forgot to tell you that every employee gets a free sandwich for lunch." I made my own sandwich and took it back home and said to Holly, "Today I made forty-eight dollars and this sandwich."

Lollipop

~

I was walking down the road one day and I saw someone that I had briefly met somewhere. He called my name, "Deepak!"

I turned around.

"Are you Deepak?"

"Yes, I am."

"My name is Sohan....remember me?"

"Yes, did I see you at the sandwich place?"

"Yes...you have a good memory."

"Thanks!"

He didn't seem to be in a hurry and it appeared as if he wanted to have a conversation with me.

"Are you still working at the same place?"

"Yes...I am, actually."

"Hmm...," he looked down and tossed a small pebble with his shoe.

I kept quiet and waited for him to look up.

"I have something to offer you…but there is a slight problem."

"Okay," I said and wondered about the offer and the problem.

"Well, I own a motel and I need a front desk manager, and the problem is that the guy you work for is my friend."

I looked at him without saying anything.

"I don't want to take away his employee, but I would like you to work for me," he looked at me and smiled. "What do you think?"

"I haven't signed any contract with him and I should be allowed to work anywhere I want," I said. "Provided I like the job."

"That's right. How about if you come and see me tomorrow at this address?"

I took his business card, which was white with blue print on it; it had a map to his motel on the backside. I went home and thought about the whole thing. I had only been working at the restaurant for three days and I wasn't enjoying it. The job at the motel seemed tempting. I had nothing to lose. I picked up the phone and called Sohan.

"Hi Sohan, this is Deepak. I was wondering if we can talk some more about the job."

"Oh, sure," he sounded happily surprised. "Why don't you come and see me at the motel?"

"Okay, what time is good for you?"

"Any time before noon is good."

I arranged to meet him at 10 in the morning the next day. I wasn't sure what to wear so I put on a dressy jacket and presented myself at his office; it was situated in his motel. He was waiting for me and greeted me when he saw me, "Hi Deepak, come on in."

"Hello."

"Would you like to see the place?"

"Sure."

He gave me a tour of his forty-room motel, which looked very basic but clean—the walls were painted grey and the floors were cement; it had a small sized parking lot in front which could accommodate about twenty cars.

I asked him, "How long have you owned this motel?"

"Long time...my father bought it thirty years ago... but you know what...it is a difficult business to be in." He took me inside the rooms and showed me the difference between queen-size and king-size beds.

I asked, "How is it difficult to be in this business?"

"I will show you how," he walked with me to another room and when he opened the door, a disgusting whiff hit my nose. Sohan pulled the bed sheet off the bed, "See...this is why." The bed sheet was covered with vomit. "People like to trash your property and we have to clean up after them."

He turned around and pointed at several empty crumpled beer cans lying under a table and said, "Come here." He took me into the bathroom and said, "Look, they treat the bathtub as a fridge." The bathtub was partially filled with ice cubes and empty beer bottles. I asked, "Why don't they use the refrigerator in the room?" He looked at me and smirked, "That is too small for them and that's why they fill the entire bathtub with ice to keep their beer chilled."

"That is not good."

"Of course not…it damages the bathtub," he sounded frustrated, "Some of these rooms smell of cigarettes, so I like to give them to people who are smokers and keep the clean ones for non-smokers."

After showing me around, he took me back to his office and asked me to sit down on an old leather couch.

"So you will be the front desk manager and you will check in the new customers and check out the leaving customers. This is mostly it. It is not a high pressure job and you can read or watch TV while you work."

It seemed like a much easier job than making sandwiches all day and cleaning dirty tables. I asked him, "Will you provide me with some training?"

"Yeah…I will work with you for an hour for the first three days…and then you will be on your own."

"Will I be the only manager in the motel?"

"Actually there is a resident manager who lives here round the clock. You can ask her if you have any questions or if you need help…let me introduce you to her," He knocked on a half-opened door in the office.

A middle-aged tired-looking Indian lady—she had dark circles around her eyes—came out. Sohan pointed at her, "This is Mira Ben," and then looked at me, "Mira

Ben…this is Deepak…our new front desk manager." Mira Ben forced a smile on her weary face and said hello. When she left, Sohan showed me how to answer the phone and how to transfer the calls to the requested rooms. He told me, "You need to pay attention and check the customer's ID—it has to be a photo ID. You don't want convicts staying here."

I looked at him with a curious face. He continued, "A driver's license is a standard form of photo ID." He pulled out his wallet from his back pocket and showed me his driver's license through the plastic cover.

"This is what it looks like…do you have one?"

"Not yet."

"Get one…you will need it."

I smiled at him and said, "I will."

After a few minutes he left and wished me good luck for the rest of the day. I was alone in the hundred-square-foot cubicle with a square hole in the wall—a counter for customers. There was a small bowl full of mint candies and lollipops on the ledge; I unwrapped one and popped it in my mouth. A few minutes later, a young black woman walked through the door. I said, "Hi! How can I help you?"

She didn't say anything, but picked up a lollipop and started unwrapping it delicately—unwinding the wrapper from the top, slowly peeling it off—looking at me and smiling mischievously.

I didn't understand what she was doing and asked again, "How can I help you?"

"You got other candies that I can work on?" She said, sucking on the lollipop, sticking it in and out, in and out, in and out of her mouth in a slow motion, and then licking it all around with her tongue.

I nervously swallowed and said, "No, these are the only candies we have."

"Alright, I am in 312, let me know if you have more candies," she said with a loud sound of lips smacking, as she pulled the lollipop out of her mouth. She left the reception area before I could say anything. While I sat there confused, thinking about what she actually wanted, Mira Ben walked into the office and said, "Don't forget to count the money before you leave."

I remembered Sohan telling me that I was supposed to count the change in the till and keep a record of the amount before I finished my shift. Counting change wasn't a big deal, but when I opened the cash register, I realized I had never counted American money—especially in a huge quantity. Seven rolls of quarters, six rolls of dimes, four rolls of nickels and the rest. It took me twenty-five minutes and four times before I got it done. Still, I was a dollar short, which I had to add from my own pocket. It was the rule. Mira Ben's tired face burst into laughter when she saw me frantically counting money and not being able to distinguish between different denominations of currency. I could spot an Indian rupee coin from a mile away and would be able to count any amount of change without even looking; I struggled to tally Uncle Sam's currency.

Mira Ben said, "Don't worry...we were like you when we first came to the US. You will learn...it takes some time." It was reassuring to hear that from her. I asked her, "When did you come to America?"

"Four years ago," she sighed.

"Do you like it here?"

"It's okay," she said and looked away with an emotionless smile.

"What do you mean?"

"Hmm...we've gone through a lot in this country."

I kept looking at her wanting to hear more.

She responded, "I have a master's degree and so does my husband...and this is what we do here."

"You don't like this job?"

"This is not a job of our choice...my husband and I have never done this kind of job...we are just passing time..."

I didn't know what to say, so I looked at her with a blank face. I could tell she wasn't finished speaking.

"We live and work here...twenty-four hours...seven days a week."

"Does that mean you can't leave?"

"One of us has to stay here...at all times," she said, sounding frustrated.

"Can't you find another job?"

"We can't because we are bound to work here until we get our green card."

Mira Ben told me that she and her husband had quit their jobs and sold their property in India to come to the

US in the hope that they would find a brighter future and good education for their children. But things didn't turn out as they had expected, and they lost their jobs. Sohan was nice enough to let them work in his motel until they got their green cards and found jobs that fit their liking. I listened to her story and it seemed that she felt better by sharing it with me.

Towards the end of the day, Sohan showed up again. He said, "I wanted to check on you…how are you doing?" I told him about the candy incident and he shook his head as if to say, "Ah, not again!"

He said, "You will get such customers every now and then…be careful."

I asked, "But, what did she want?"

"She just wanted a free room."

I still didn't get it, but said, "Okay."

Sohan asked, "How did things go, other than that?"

I told him that I dealt with three more customers after that incident. All of them inquired about the room and the charges…they checked in and none of them asked for candies.

Night Shift

~

One day while browsing the web, I half-heartedly applied for a job at a local TV station in Charlottesville. At this point, I had filled out hundreds of job applications and had never heard from most of the places; I didn't think that I had much chance of getting this TV job. But, to my surprise, when I returned home after a stroll, I saw the red flashing light on my answering machine. I pressed the button to listen to the message. It was a young girl's voice who said, "I am looking for Mr. Deepak Singh—" My first reaction was to delete it without listening to the whole thing; I had been getting a lot of junk calls from companies who wanted to sell me calling cards for India—I thought it would have been one of those callers. But, I decided to listen to the full message. The message was from the TV station and she asked me to call back to schedule an interview. I couldn't believe it was true and listened to the message four times and frantically looked for a pen to write down the phone number to call back.

I immediately phoned back Maria, the lady at the station, "Hello, my name is Deepak Singh and I got a call from your station."

"Oh yes…this is Maria. Thanks for calling Mr. Singh. When do you think you can come for an interview?"

"I can come today if you want," I said eagerly.

"Sure, how about at 10 am?"

"That sounds good…I will see you soon."

I was too excited to schedule the interview any other day, and was afraid that if I gave them too much time, they might change their minds and drop the idea of interviewing me. I quickly got dressed up and went to the place. I arrived at a building with a huge tower built next to it and several white vans that had dish antenna mounted on top, parked in the parking lot in front of the building. A short young woman greeted me with a smile and said, "Are you here for the interview?"

"Yes, that's right."

"Come in my office."

She offered me a seat and pulled herself up on her chair holding on to its hand rest—she was no more than five feet tall. She looked at me and twinkled her eyes and said, "So….why do you want this job?"

It all happened so quickly that I didn't have much time to prepare for the interview. After a few seconds of thinking I said, "I have a radio background so I thought it would be a good opportunity to work in television."

She didn't ask me anything about my radio work experience and jumped to a different question; she looked down at my CV and said, "We use a lot of computerized equipment here...how do you feel about that?"

"I know how to use computers and I am willing to learn new things."

She smiled and asked me, "Can you drive?" I was surprised at that question and said, "I can. I didn't think this job required driving."

"It doesn't, but we like to hire people who can drive."

It didn't make sense to me. She wrapped up the interview in less than ten minutes and said, "Okay...we need to do a drug test."

"Drug test...why?"

"Yes, a drug test...it is mandatory. We don't hire people who consume drugs....you have to go to this doctor," she handed me a paper with an address and a map drawn at the bottom of it, "and you don't have to pay anything." I had never taken drugs or gone through any drug test in my life. It felt strange that someone asked for it—it was like being accused of doing something wrong. I took the paper from her and left the building. I went straight to the doctor after the interview. The lady doctor who appeared to be in her early forties said to me, "We will need your urine sample." I said, "Okay." She took me to a bathroom which was ten feet away and said, "Go, pee in that toilet." I looked at her and thought it was strange that she walked me to the bathroom, as if I would have lost my way if she hadn't come with me. She said again, "Get inside!" I walked into the bathroom while she kept standing there looking at me. As I started to close the bathroom door she said, "No...no...no...leave it open."

Not only had I never taken a drug test before, but I had never urinated in front of a woman. I had peed on many Indian walls in public, but a woman never stopped to take a look. It was a very awkward moment. I didn't know what to say to her. I remembered my college days in Lucknow, when the senior students would make the newcomers do embarrassing things—dance in public, give a flower to a random girl, run with no shirt on—but I couldn't recall asking any of them to urinate in front of a woman.

I turned my back to the woman and slowly unzipped my pants, hoping she would turn her face away. I did my business with my eyes closed and as soon as I zipped up, I heard, "Alright, now...do not flush the toilet," –she was there the whole time. I came out of the bathroom with my eyes watching my feet. She handed me a piece of paper and told me that they would send the results to the TV station. After coming out of the doctor's office, I realized that I had driven four miles just to urinate. It felt awkward to be doing this in a country where most businesses strive to be quick and easy, provide at-your-door-service and make their motto *You Want It We Got It*. How come they never came up with the idea of a drive-thru peeing facility or an online ordering system where you could Fed-Ex your urine sample to the doctor's clinic?

A few days later, I saw a message from Maria on my answering machine, "I was just calling to let you know that your drug test came out negative. We would like you to schedule the second interview." I called back and decided on a date for the next meeting. She handed me a set of papers to read about the company and then sign at the bottom. After I read the literature, she smiled and asked me, "So when would you like to start?" I couldn't believe that I was actually being offered a job—a job where I didn't have to cut bread or deal with rude customers, but something I really liked and had some knowledge about. I told Maria that I would be willing to start as soon as possible. She said, "How about next Monday at 12?" When I said yes, she told me to report to Ted—the station engineer. I agreed and went back home feeling incredibly happy and enjoyed the rest of the days until Monday.

Monday arrived and I showed up at 12 pm. I didn't see Maria in her office. I sat down on a couch in the lobby and saw people pass by looking busy, wearing formal clothing. I waited for Maria to come and introduce me to Ted. After ten minutes, when I didn't see Maria, I stopped a young looking guy and told him that I was supposed to start work that day and report to Ted. He looked at me with a quizzical face and wrinkled his forehead and said, "Hmm…Ted's doesn't get here until 8 pm. Did they really tell you to come at 12 pm?"

"Yes," I said.

The guy fixed his tie and said, "Let me check," and went inside a door. He came back with a grin on his face and said, "Apparently someone told you the wrong time. You were supposed to come at 12 am." I found it hard to believe my ears and exclaimed, "In the night?"

"Yes, your shift starts at 12 am. You will work 12 to 8."

I was taken aback and felt cheated. Maria hadn't mentioned the time of day at all. I had never worked at night; I became very sad to hear about my shift hours. I wasn't sure if I could do this. The guy saw my face turn sad in an instant and said, "I know man…it sucks…we have not been able to retain people for this shift."

It started to become clear why they called me for the interview and offered me the job so quickly. But, it was too late. I had gone through the interview process and I had not been working a good job for a long time; I had nothing to lose. I told the guy that I would come at 12 am. I went back home and thought about the whole thing. When I had told Holly about the job, she was very happy that I was finally getting a break and was going to start work. I didn't have the heart to tell her the bad news. I finally told her about the hours; her face fell immediately. I could tell that she wanted me to work and get some experience, but at the same time she didn't want me to leave her alone every night. We both decided that I should give it a try.

Around 10 pm when it was time for us to go to bed, I still had two more hours before I started work for that day. Holly suggested I take a short nap before I left for the night. I didn't want to wear my pajamas to bed since

I was afraid I might never wake up. So, I dressed up—put on my shirt, pants, belt, and shoes—and then lay next to Holly. Before we fell deeply asleep, Holly woke me up, "You have to go to work." I looked at the clock—it was 11:30 pm—and told her that I still had a few more minutes. Finally, I got up and washed my face and said good night to Holly; I hated leaving her in the night.

I drove in the dark; it was a cold foggy night and the only way to tell there were other cars on the road was by seeing their headlights, which were weakened by the dense fog. As I approached the TV station, I noticed that other vehicles were leaving the premises. I heard people saying good night to each other—their day was over, mine had just begun. I walked to the main entrance to enter the building but it had been shut for the night. The place looked very different from what I had seen at 12 pm—all the lights were off in the lobby; the only light there was coming through a crack in the door. I made hand gestures through the glass door when someone walked by. He came out and led me through a side door inside the building, into a long hallway-like room. All of a sudden I was surrounded by bright lights, men dressed in suits and ties, girls with pearls, wearing mascara, crisp miniskirts and matching tops—looking wide awake at midnight. One whole length of the wall was studded with TV screens playing different things. Below the televisions were extra large flat screen computers—with green and blue rows and columns—lined up on a long and narrow table. I was asked to sit and wait for Ted to show up. I pulled out a chair and started watching one of the TV screens which featured a young lady reading the local news. I watched the news for a couple of minutes and it occurred to me that I had seen the announcer on the TV somewhere. I noticed a woman standing next to me watching the same screen; she had an arresting resemblance to the woman on the TV, except that her face looked much bigger. While I looked at her from the corner of my eye, someone wearing a headset and a microphone came up to her and said, "Kristy, we gotta record that again…you mispronounced a word."

She responded, "I know…I just saw that…yeah, let's do it again." She followed the man into a different room. I realized that she was actually the same woman as on the TV. It was amazing. I felt important that I was going to work with local celebrities.

After about ten minutes a six-foot-tall man, who had long blond hair tied with a rubber band, round steel-framed glasses and a long flowing beard which was divided in two halves at the chin, came to me and said, "Are you Deepak?"

I stood up from my chair and said, "Yes, I am. Are you Ted?"

"Yes I am…I apologize for the mix-up with your timing."

"It's okay…I wasn't quite prepared to work at this time."

"No shit man…fucking graveyard shift…everybody hates it…but we gotta keep the show goin'."

I was surprised to hear him use swear words on our first meeting. I wasn't sure if he was angry with me or if he had had a bad day and I happened to be the one to bear the brunt.

"Alright my man...let me explain what you are supposed to do here," he said and started walking in the opposite direction. I followed him. "So, you will be working on three motherfucking stations, which means you will have to watch three computer screens—simultaneously," he explained and then paused for a second and turned to me, "I am sorry my man...do you swear?" I wanted to tell him I did swear but not at work and not with co-workers and definitely not when meeting someone for the first time. Instead, I smiled in response to his question. "You are my man," he said with a big grin. I smiled again. He quickly put his arm around my shoulders and said, "Listen...if anyone gives you a hard time here...let me know, okay...I will kick some ass for ya." I said okay. But so far, the only person I was having a hard time with was him.

He continued with his instructions, "Basically what you have to do is insert advertisements between shows. You gotta be attentive because if you miss putting in an ad the companies call and yell at us—we can't afford that since we need their money." He pointed a finger at me said, "And the most important thing...we switch from local telecast to national telecast at 6 am...if you don't do that people will be watching a black screen on their TVs in Charlottesville."

By the time I got done talking with Ted, everybody had left for the day, except me and one other person. Ted introduced me to him, "Charlie, this is Deepak," he turned to me, "Deepak this is Charlie...you two will be running the show tonight."

It was around 1 am now. If I wasn't working here, I would be deep asleep in my bed. Instead, my senses had been shaken by the razzmatazz in the station and Ted's effortless use of swear words. I wondered if he did that on purpose to make sure that I stayed awake throughout the night. I took my seat and started inserting advertisements every time a show ended. It seemed like an easy job; I was getting paid to sit in a very comfortable chair and watch TV, except that I never did this at home at 2 am. I was getting to see a different America in a different setting. I was also getting to see very different kinds of shows on TV—ones that I had never seen before during the day.

I managed to stay awake until four in the morning, but started having trouble keeping my eyes open after that. I was in bad shape by 6 am and at seven in the morning, Charlie had to tap on my shoulder several times to stop me from hitting my head on the desk. He would say, "You alright, dude?" I shook my head, walked around a little and then came back to my seat to nod off again. I struggled to make it through; the time between 7 and 8 am seemed like the longest hour of my life.

I left the station as soon as the clock hit 8. I walked out to the car and realized that I wasn't awake enough to be able to drive home—it took me a few minutes to get the car key into the lock correctly. I decided to stop for a cup of coffee at a cafeteria near the station. I bought the coffee and as I started adding milk and sugar to it, I heard a girl in the shop saying, "Hey, Jessica...did you watch the morning news today?"

The other girl replied, "No, why?"

"You know...I was watching TV this morning and all of a sudden the screen went black...there was nothing on it...for SEVEN minutes."

I quickly walked out of the store.

White Stuff

~

After being in America for a couple of months, it was time to meet my wife's family. Holly had met all my folks in India, but I had not met any of my in-laws so far. As a son-in-law of color, I did not know what to expect. I knew if I had married an Indian girl of my parents' choice, I would have gotten very special treatment on my first visit to her family. As a *Damad*, a son-in-law of an Indian family, I would get the best of everything—best food, best chair, best bed and all the brothers and sisters of the bride would be on duty to attend to my every desire, making sure I was comfortable.

I wasn't sure how Holly's family would treat me. I didn't know what was expected of me as a new member of the family. I could tell Holly was nervous about introducing me to her people and taking me to her village, but she didn't make it apparent. She was the first person to marry a non-white person in her family and none of them had been around people from other countries. I was anxious.

Since Holly's parents live separately and have small houses, we were going to stay with her grandparents. This made me feel better since I had gotten to know Gram and Papa better than anyone else in Holly's family; I had talked to them several time on the phone and exchanged emails.

We started preparing for our trip. This was the first time I was going to Pennsylvania; I was excited about seeing another part of America, but uneasy about meeting my in-laws. It was going to be a long drive from Charlottesville to Brockway, Pennsylvania. Holly was going to drive the whole way—I had never driven in America before—and she wanted us to leave early in the morning. It was late November and the temperature was around 30 degree Fahrenheit, causing the plants to be covered in frost. We started the car at six in the morning, about twenty minutes before we were supposed to leave, so that the windshield and the windows would be defrosted.

We packed some food and got a bottle of water ready for the journey. We were supposed to carry heavy woolens to be prepared for the Pennsylvania weather. We left Charlottesville after the car engine warmed up. We were going to drive north for about 325 miles and according to MapQuest it was going to take 5 hours and 49 minutes without stops. The first major highway we came across was I-64. Holly wanted me to keep updating her about the approaching exits. The last time I travelled on a highway was when I first arrived in the country, I was exhausted from the seventeen hour plane journey. This time my mind was fresh and I was prepared to enjoy the ride and the scenic views along the way. As we approached the highway Holly pressed on the gas pedal to make the car go 65 miles per hour, following the speed limit on the highway. Sixty-five miles an hour translates to an outrageous speed of 105 kilometers per hour. In India, when I drove my scooter anything above 40 miles per hour, people on the street looked at me as if I was on a suicidal mission and the scooter's engine sounded like someone was playing a cheap radio on full volume.

I looked at the speedometer in the car and the needle was fixed on 65, as if it was glued to that number. I asked Holly if it was working since the needle hadn't moved for the last fifteen minutes. She told me, "Since we are going to be on this highway for a long time, I set the car on cruise-control mode...it will stay on this speed as long as I don't use the brakes." I wasn't aware of that feature, and I couldn't imagine using it in India. I had never been on a road where I didn't have to change my vehicle's speed every two minutes; there were too many distractions on the road, making you slow down at a moment's notice.

Holly's car—a big American car—didn't make any noise and 65 miles an hour didn't seem very fast sitting inside it. People in other vehicles on the road would come up and drive along parallel to our car for several minutes before one of us got ahead or changed lanes. Often times I saw—I would take a peek into their cars when they came close—people in other cars doing several other things apart from driving: talking on the phone, looking in the mirror to fix their makeup, eating a sandwich with one hand and sipping soda out of the other. Since we were driving at almost the same speed as other people, our car seemed parked next to others.

After driving for about two hours we were greeted by a sign saying, *Welcome to West Virginia*; we thought it was time to fill up the gas tank and stretch our legs. We pulled into a gas fuelling station at a very festive-looking gas station called *Sheetz*. She told me that she had worked as a cashier at a different *Sheetz*, located in her town, a few years ago. She also mentioned that almost every cousin in her family has worked there at some point in their lives. We topped up our fuel tank and went inside the building to use the restrooms and get something to eat. The red-colored gas station had all its employees dressed in blue. Country music was pouring out of the little circular vents in the ceiling in every corner of the premises, even in the restroom. One of the songs caught my attention; it was John Denver:

> *Almost heaven, West Virginia*
> *Blue Ridge Mountains*
> *Shenandoah river*
> *Life is old there...*
> *Older than the trees*
> *Younger than the mountains*
> *Growing like a breeze*
> *Country roads, take me home*
> *To the place I belong*

The song had become popular among my friends in college in India. Back then, I used to sing it all the time but had never imagined that I would be living near the Blue Ridge Mountains in the Shenandoah Valley and riding through West Virginia. It was ironic that I was travelling on country roads in West Virginia but they were not taking me home—although they were calling my wife home—and I definitely didn't belong to the place. Instead, I was ten thousand miles away from home.

We bought coffee and a glazed donut—donuts were something I fell in love with on my first day in America; it came close to Indian *Jalebi*, fried dough dipped in a sugar solution—and got back on the road. We drove through some of the most beautiful parts of Virginia. The roads curved around the mountains and uphill, offering some breathtaking views; it seemed like our car had entered a painting—wide roads with neatly mowed grassy dividers and rolling hills on both sides. Every now and then we saw big bales of hay scattered around and cows with big white and black patches grazing in the lush green fields, surrounded by white wooden fences. Clouds allowed the sun to fall on the hills in an uneven fashion, causing some parts to appear bright green and others to look dark.

It started getting difficult to maintain the speed and maneuver on twisty roads—West Virginia had a 70-mile-per-hour speed limit. After driving for a while we entered the state of Maryland and crossed a bridge that was built over the Potomac. It suddenly got louder as we got on the bridge; the bridge was built with concrete, which caused the car tires to make a different sound. The river looked calm under it.

Apart from admiring the scenery and gawking at other people in their cars, I kept offering snacks and changing the music on the car stereo while Holly concentrated on driving. After a little while I saw something in the rearview mirror that I hadn't seen in the last two months in America—a group of motorcyclists. Even though it was a bright sunny day, they had their headlights turned on and kept coming closer as I saw in the rearview mirror. In a matter of a few seconds, our car was surrounded by half a dozen giant roaring engines mounted on steel frames, tucked between two fat wheels. Their vehicles were at least four times bigger and bulkier than the biggest motorcycle I had ever seen in India. The handlebars rose two feet above the gas tank and the footrest was placed only a few inches below the headlights, making the drivers' limbs look like they were sticking up in the air. The fuel tanks were as big as a camel's hump and the wheels looked like they belonged to a tractor. As they slowly cruised past our car, I noticed that most of the bikes were Harley Davidsons. The motorcyclists seemed to be middle-aged, most of them had pony tails and sported leather jackets with flames, an eagle, or a skull painted on them. The presence of several Harleys roaring around our car made Holly nervous; she couldn't decide whether she should change lanes, slow down, or speed up. Since all of them were going faster than us, they soon disappeared with their brake lights twinkling, making them look like red traffic lights from a distance. It wasn't clear if they were a group or individuals who just happened to be going in the same direction.

After driving through the state of Maryland for a while we took Route 522 and entered the quaint little town of Berkeley Springs in West Virginia. It had only one street. There was one gas station and every other building on that street seemed to be a spa salon. We filled our gas tank at *Sheetz* one more time. This was the second *Sheetz* I had been to on our journey and I was already falling in love with it. Its color scheme, its employees, its layout, its clean bathroom and its music were enchanting. I liked it so much that I started looking forward to stopping at the next one.

After driving for a while we encountered heavy traffic; a lot of it consisted of bright red colored trucks with shiny stainless steel rearview mirrors attached to each side of the doors. The size of the trucks made our car look like an ant. They kept passing us from both sides. While I was amazed by their enormity and looked out the window, Holly's forehead wrinkled with stress; I could tell she wasn't enjoying driving between thirty foot-long and forty-foot high trucks. We noticed a truck in front of us had his left signal blinking. We waited for him to change lanes for a few minutes, but he continued driving in the same lane, and indicating that he wanted to change lanes. We decided to pass him. As our car passed his truck, I looked up in the driver's seat in an effort to make eye contact with the driver. A white face with red stubble looked down as if he was on a tall cliff and I was sitting fifty feet below. I gestured with my hands that his turn signal was on. He honked at me to say thanks for telling him.

After a couple more hours of driving we entered the state of Pennsylvania—the place where my wife grew up. After driving for a few more miles, I saw a car in front of us driving about ten miles slower than the speed limit. There was a man driving the car and a woman with long hair was sitting in the passenger seat. A few minutes later the woman unbuckled herself from the safety belt and disappeared. The man in the car slowed down even more than before and started drifting from one lane to the other. The woman appeared again after about five miles. I tried asking my wife about what was going on in front of us, but she changed the topic immediately and said, "What's the next exit we have to take?" I looked down on the map to tell her about the next exit number.

While I was still confused, and wondering why the people in the car in front were acting funny, I saw a sign that said, "Intercourse". I pinched myself to see if I was dreaming. I had never imagined a town could be called Intercourse. I am not sure how my father would react if I told him I was going to "Intercourse". Soon the people ahead of us got off at the next exit. I wondered if Intercourse was their destination.

The temperature plummeted with every mile we drove in Pennsylvania; I could feel it by touching the ice-cold windshield. About eighty miles before Holly's village, I noticed the earth had a strange texture and the color was different—white and grayish. I asked Holly, "What is that white stuff?"

She said, "Where?"

"There, by the side of the road."

"That's snow," she responded.

I exclaimed in disbelief, "Snow!"

I had never seen snow before and couldn't believe that I was actually seeing it. I quickly rolled down the window glass to get a better view. Everything got whiter and the temperature got colder as we moved further into the state of Pennsylvania. We passed some more towns along the way—Altoona, Philipsburg, Dubois—and soon I saw a sign, BROCKWAY 8. The sign made my heart race. I had been enjoying my journey up until then and none of the other towns made me feel like that. I had been told so many stories about Brockway and I had been to this village in my dreams so many times that the actual sight of the big green sign made me nervous about being there in reality. It was actually happening—I was only eight miles away from meeting my wife's family, only eight miles away from visiting her home where she grew up, only eight miles away from where everything was familiar to her and everything new to me. It started to sink in that I was actually very close to my *sasural*, my in-laws' place. How will people react to me? How will I react to everyone? What kind of questions will they ask? How will everything turn out? I was getting overwhelmed by so many thoughts.

The road to Brockway meandered through a residential area with houses on both sides. The yellow stripe on the road disappeared and the overgrown bushes on the side brushed our car as we drove along on a narrow path. We came upon a small tunnel-like passage where we had to slow down to let the cars coming from the other direction pass through. After a few miles we arrived at a T intersection where Holly stopped the car at a stop sign which was perched on a wooden stick, buried three quarters in snow. She shifted the gear to bring the car into park mode and pulled the visor down to block the sun, which was sitting very low in the sky, creating long tree shadows in the snow covered field in front of us. Looking at my worried face, she gently grabbed my shirt and pulled me towards her and gave me a kiss and said, "You will be fine." Wearing a faint smile on her face she continued looking into my eyes for a few minutes before we moved again.

Farm Life

~

A couple of minutes later we arrived at our destination and pulled the car into the driveway of a lonely looking house sitting on a huge farm. We parked the car in front of a white garage door. The house had dark red brick outer walls and on the second story there was a window that had a flowerpot on the sill.

I got out of the car and looked around. There were huge open spaces all around the house and there were only three other houses in the vicinity—everything else was an open field, covered with a sheet of snow with yellow grass peeking out here and there. All four houses had American flags hoisted on poles in their front yards. While I was still stretching my arms and legs, a small white door opened and a young red-haired boy, wearing a checkered flannel shirt and a pair of faded-blue jeans, came out. Holly told me that he was her youngest cousin, Aaron. He appeared to be in his early teens. I shook hands with him and he gave me a smile; I noticed that he was shy and uncomfortable making eye contact with me. A minute later, an elderly couple came out. Since we were going to stay at Holly's grandparents and I had seen their pictures before, I knew who they were. Holly had mentioned to me earlier that I could call them Gram and Papa—that's how she addressed them. Gram was wearing a white sweater that had flowers knitted on it and a pair of loose jeans. She had short curly light brown hair and a pair of eyeglasses sat on her nose. She smiled and gave me a hug while Papa took a picture of his wife hugging me and Holly. He wore a flannel shirt and a pair of jeans and eyeglasses that covered half of his face; he had his hair swooped up from the side.

Aaron helped us carry our luggage inside the house. We walked into an area that looked like an office, with a desk, computer, a couple of printers and a photocopier neatly arranged in a small space. There were pictures of different cars on the wall, arranged in an interesting order. Seeing me show interest in the pictures, Gram paused for a minute and said, "These are the cars we have owned over the years."

I asked, "How many years?"

She shook her head as if to think and said, "Ah, about forty…"

As we walked in, Gram mentioned that we were in the basement of the house, although it was on the same level as the road. We moved ahead and climbed a set of creaky wooden stairs and arrived at the first floor. Gram showed us the room she had gotten ready for us. It had a very bouncy bed with a white and furry bedsheet neatly spread on it. A dresser rested against the wall in front and a closet by the side of the bed. I laid our luggage down on the floor and walked through the hallway to come to the living room where a couch, a wooden rocking chair, a red recliner, a blue recliner, and a television set were placed around a fireplace. A wall next to the fireplace had several portraits of family members—I recognized Holly, her mom and her brother. I asked Gram about some of the people I didn't know and she explained, "That's John, my youngest son and those are his sons, Don and Aaron, who you just met…and that's my older son Roger and his family…" She gave a detailed description of the people on the wall.

It was cozy and warm inside, but I could see the snow covered fields through the large glass windows in the living room. Papa was sitting in the red recliner. A small round table with some magazines, a lamp and a cordless phone were within arm's reach. It seemed to me as if it was his corner, where he sat most of the time. When everyone settled down, he said, "You guys made it in a pretty good time." Holly said, "Yeah, route 81 wasn't bad today." He responded, "Hmm," as if he was surprised and happy at the same time.

Gram noticed I was still standing and wasn't sure where to sit; she said, "Feel free to sit anywhere you want and do anything you like…treat it like your own home." It was very nice of her to say that. I thanked her and sat down next to Holly on the couch. Gram came and pulled up a lever by the side of the couch which made my legs come up straight in a quick motion. "You can use this to put up your legs and relax," she said and smiled. I wasn't expecting my legs to move on their own, but it felt nice to be able to stretch.

After a few minutes of talking, Gram announced that it was supper time—Holly had told me earlier that her grandparents eat dinner at 5 pm. On asking why they ate so early, Papa explained, "Farmers get hungry when they return from the field after a hard day's work." He told me he grew up on a farm and considers his wife as a farm wife; before he retired he worked as a school teacher, but found time to work in his fields during his summer vacation. I looked through the window and his farm stretched as far as my eyes could see. I thought of my uncles—my father's brothers—in my village, who were school teachers and also farmers. They used to take me to their fields to show me different vegetables they grew and taught me how to divide and multiply numbers when I went to see them in my—and their—summer vacation.

While I was still lost in thoughts, everyone started moving to the dining area that was next to the kitchen. There was a china plate and a drinking glass placed in front of each of the six chairs. Papa picked up a jar full of milk and started pouring into every glass. Gram and Holly passed food through an opening between the stove and the cupboards to the dining table. Before we sat down two more people—Holly's Uncle John and his son Don—showed up at the table. I shook hands with them and they returned a friendly smile. John was wearing overalls that were partially covered with sawdust—I remembered Holly telling me he was a carpenter. Don had shoulder length red hair and he seemed to be in his late teens.

Before we started eating, Gram bowed her head and folded her hands to say a prayer; everyone closed their eyes. She thanked God that Holly and I made a safe journey home and said that we were blessed to eat together. As we began eating, I tried to be polite to everyone by offering them a chair before I took one and kept asking if I could pass them anything—salt, pepper, ketchup and butter, etc. Holly poked her elbow in my ribs gently and whispered, "Don't worry about anyone…just eat."

I grew up in a household where I was told to respect my elders—offer to let them sit before I sat myself, leave my chair and stand up if they walked in the room, ask them if they need anything—and I was trying to do the same thing here. I noticed that I was the only person looking out for Holly's grandparents and her uncle while the others were busy eating.

Holly's grandmother passed me a huge tray full of thick slices of meat. I asked Holly quietly about what kind of meat it was. She whispered again, "Beef!" I subtly pushed the tray away with the back of my index finger, making sure no one saw. I looked at other options on the table, another tray full of meat, and asked my wife again, "What's that?"

She said, "That is ham."

I said keeping my voice low, "You mean, pig?"

She looked at me—as if to say I shouldn't expect to get my mother's chicken curry at her grandmother's home—and said, "Eat this, this is mashed potato," pointing at a plate with a mound of white pulp on it.

I realized I couldn't eat any of the meat available on the table; I had never eaten any of it before. If my mother found out that I had eaten beef—sacred cow—she would probably never let me in her kitchen again. I remember on a day of *Puja*, a Hindu religious ritual, she wouldn't allow anyone in her kitchen without washing their hands. She didn't let anyone eat non-vegetarian food on those days.

So, at the dining table in Brockway, I was confined to mashed potatoes. I enjoyed eating it but it was very different from my mother's *alloo ka bharta;* she would mash the potatoes and mix in spices, green chilies, garlic, and salt. The dish on the table was just potatoes and butter mashed together. I had to dose it with salt and pepper to add some taste. Others were ripping apart the thick slices of meat with their knives and forks and stuffing their mouths with big chunks. Every two or three minutes, I would hear someone say, "Salt please!—pepper please!" I took it that none of the dishes had salt or pepper in them—everything was just boiled, or roasted with no spices at all. It then dawned on me that the dining area and the kitchen didn't reek of any spices. I understood why. I figured I was going to have to make do with bland food for the rest of my time in Pennsylvania. It was my first day there and I was already craving *Dal,* spicy lentil soup.

When my mother cooked, her spices sometimes made me come out of my room coughing with tears in my eyes.

My mother would look at me and giggle and tell me that she was roasting cumin seeds for *Dahi Vada*; she knew I loved deep fried dough dipped in salty yoghurt. The whole house reeked of spices; even the neighbors could tell by the smell that something delicious was being prepared in the Singh household.

After we finished eating supper, Gram said, "There's dessert, too." She picked up a white rectangular box and set it on the dining table. It was full of blue, orange, and red cookies in the shape of a leaf or a flower. I ate one and liked it a lot. When I asked her where she got them from, she replied, "Oh no…I bake 'em myself." She didn't know that I had a sweet tooth and that I wouldn't shy away from any kind of sweets. I ate half of those cookies in no time. I wished she could teach my mother to make cookies and learn to make Indian food from her.

After we finished eating, everyone moved back to the living room and sat on the couch to watch TV. Gram and Holly talked while Papa dozed off on his recliner. I started feeling sleepy so I said good night to everyone and crawled into the cozy bed Gram had prepared for us.

The Harvest Festival

~

The next day was the American festival of Thanksgiving and Roger—one of Holly's uncles—was hosting the dinner to celebrate it at his house; he lived across the road from Gram and Papa's place. A lot of Holly's relatives—cousins, brother, mother, uncles, aunts, and various other people—were supposed to gather to eat and party. I started getting uneasy at the thought of meeting so many of her relatives. I had heard from my friends in India about how unnerving it was to meet their wives' families for the first time. Since my wife and her family were Americans with a totally different cultural background than mine, I was feeling extremely terrified. I had prepared myself to meet her family members one by one, but wasn't ready to tackle them all at once. When we got ready to go to the party, Papa drove us in his van from his garage to Uncle Roger's driveway—a distance of less than fifty meters. When I asked him if we could walk, he said, "Get in the van...it's easier this way." We arrived at Uncle Roger's house in less than twenty seconds; the car engine didn't even get to warm up before it was turned off again. There were many cars parked in his driveway. I wondered if people from the other two houses in the neighborhood drove too. Uncle Roger's house was a newer looking building and had grey siding. There was a smaller house on wheels parked in his garage. On enquiring, Holly explained that it was a recreational vehicle and Uncle Roger used it when he wanted go on a vacation. The vehicle was designed to resemble a home with a built-in bed, couch, TV, and a kitchen with all the modern facilities.

We entered his house and were greeted by the host. He shook my hand and said, "Welcome to the family." Uncle Roger was a handsome-looking man with a square jaw and grey hair. He took my jacket and hung it on a hanger tucked behind the door. The house looked plush—leather sofas, rosewood piano, a big flat screen TV on the wall, spacious kitchen with a black granite top island in the middle—it looked like a suite in a five star hotel. The basement of the house had a play area for kids and an entertainment center. The entire house was carpeted. It blew my mind to see a house equipped with such modern conveniences in the middle of a wilderness—surrounded by miles and miles of empty land.

The house was full with people. A lot of them were Holly's cousins, who were mostly teenagers. People were talking in small groups around the house—the cousins were joking and laughing among themselves, Gram and

Papa were talking with one of their friends, Uncle Roger and his wife were socializing with Holly. Although people were friendly towards me, I found it hard to mingle and couldn't decide which group I should associate with. I didn't have anything in common with anyone. I was not getting any of the jokes that Holly's cousins were having fun with and couldn't participate in any of the gossip with older people. Soon it was time to eat. People started gathering around a long table covered with a red table cloth; shiny spoons, forks and knives were neatly organized in front of every chair. Some of the family members started bringing food from the kitchen to the table. Within minutes the table was covered with a variety of dishes, most of which I had never seen before. I asked Holly, who was sitting next to me, to explain the different dishes. She said, "Sure," pointing at a giant looking roasted bird, "that's turkey," she continued, "that's turkey stuffing and that is the gravy, that's mashed potatoes, this is cranberry sauce, and that is green bean casserole." After a brief pause she said, "Oh yeah…that is the best part…Gram's pumpkin pie and I don't know who brought that, but that is a pecan pie...good stuff."

After a short prayer, everyone started eating. People talked while eating, making comments about how good the food was and that it was going to be a cold winter that year, that sort of thing. Although Holly's family was very nice, no one made an effort to start a conversation with me. They didn't seem to notice or acknowledge that an Indian was sitting amongst them—the only brown person in the house—and celebrating a major American festival for the first time, ever. I was expecting that everyone would inundate me with hundreds of questions about India, my background, my family, etc. It didn't happen at all. I felt awkward being the only one not talking, but continued eating and tried to show interest in their conversations.

We spent the whole afternoon at Uncle Roger's and returned when it started to get dark. An hour or so after getting back, everyone sat around the fireplace and watched TV. Gram made herself a cup of coffee and asked me if I wanted some. I requested tea. She brought a round tin box full of different kinds of teas—lemon tea, raspberry tea, green tea, herbal tea—and asked me to pick one. I chose lemon tea.

Gram came and sat down next to me with her cup of coffee. I asked her about the origin of Thanksgiving about its meaning and she explained that it is a harvest festival celebrated to give thanks for the harvest. She questioned me about the festivals in India and it led us to talk for hours. I soon realized that I was able to share my feelings and thoughts with her easily. I hadn't been able to do this with anyone else until then in the US. I was curious about everything and had many questions. Holly would often get tired of me asking her about everything and she wouldn't always explain things clearly. I was able to ask any question and Gram responded in detail. I used to share my thoughts and opinions and ask other people's opinions with my friends and family in India, but in America, I noticed that people wouldn't respond to my questions clearly. They would often get quiet or shrug their shoulders as if they didn't know what to say when I asked about family, race, relationships, or some other delicate issue. They were not very open about sharing their thoughts or opinions about such matters, but they would talk endlessly about something superficial like a TV show, a football game, cars or food. Gram asked me serious questions and answered my questions clearly, saying what she thought. My mother is quite like her in that respect. She wouldn't hesitate to express her opinion. If anyone irked her, she would make sure they knew she was unhappy.

I asked Gram about her house and how old it was; she pulled out an old video cassette and showed me a detailed film that she had made when the house was being built. She explained the whole process of building the house. She told me that the house was built in 1969—the year she got married to Papa, several years after the death of her first husband. It was interesting to see that the house had a lot of modern amenities—an intercom, central heating, an automatic garage door—even though it was built four decades ago. I asked her, "Gram, where did you live before this house was built?" She said, "Oh…I lived in Beachwoods, about three miles from here. And, before that I grew up in Hormtown, which is about ten miles from here…you know the school I attended there has been converted into a community center now and that's where we have Christmas parties sometimes." I was amazed to know that she had spent all her life within a radius of fifteen miles. I asked her if she knew a lot of people in Brockway. She said, "Oh yeah…I know almost everyone…Brockway is not all that big."

I noticed that she had a different way of pronouncing certain words. She would insert the letter R in certain words and replace the letter O with the letter A in others. She took me into another section of her living room where I saw an old piano sitting in a corner. I asked her, "Gram, who plays the piano?"

She replied, "Oh my gorsh….it is an old piana, I used to sit by the winda and play…I still play but not as much as I used to…let me go warsh my hands and I will play something for ya."

I loved the way she spoke and showed me things and explained where they came from and how she acquired them. A lot of things in her house were older than me. She pointed at a billiards table in the basement and said, "That is forty years old and we bought it through *Deals on Wheels*. I didn't know what *Deals on Wheels* was so I asked her. She said, "It was a program on radio that was popular starting about forty years ago. People advertised various things…and you had to call them if you liked any of their stuff."

After she showed me some more things in the house, she dug out an old accordion from her closet. She strapped it to her shoulders and started playing and singing, *"You are my sunshine, my only sunshine, you make me happy when skies are grey…you'll never know dear, how much I love you, please don't take my sunshine away…"* I thought it was very sweet of her to sing for me. Talking to my grandmother in-law made me feel like a human again; I had had enough of living away from family.

Gram was the first person who asked me about my family and she was curious to know about my life in

India. She showed interest in life in India, in general. I was delighted to tell her what I did in India, about my father, mother, brother and sister. I had been waiting for someone to ask me all this. We both were eager to tell our stories and also to listen to each other's tales. Since she grew up on a farm, she had great interest in agriculture. She took me out to her kitchen garden behind her house and showed me various vegetables she had grown. She also asked me if India had similar plants. Some of them looked close to what I had seen in India but had different names. She opened her refrigerator and showed me the various jars of pickles she had prepared—all from the produce that came from her garden. Looking at her pickles made me think of my mother; every year she made different kinds of pickles—mango, lemon, red pepper. It was strange that I was talking to my grandmother in-law ten thousand miles away from home, in a different country, different climate, different lifestyle, but she still reminded me of my mother. My mother and Holly's grandmother spoke different languages, ate different food, celebrated different festivals, but still had so much in common.

After walking around the house with her for a while, she told me she makes maple syrup with her younger son, Tim, and sells it in the neighborhood. I had never heard of it before so I asked, "What is maple syrup?"

She explained, "Maple trees store sugar in their roots… we tap it and concentrate it and then it can be eaten with pancakes…waffles and oatmeal."

"Are these trees found all over America?"

"No, they are mostly found in cold climates...Canada is a big producer of maple syrup." She showed me a bottle filled with maple syrup; the label had the shape of a leaf. After looking at it for a few minutes I recognized that it was the same leaf as the one on the Canadian flag. We walked out together and she pointed at a house across the street and said, "That's my son Roger's house. He is a carpenter," and then she turned in the other direction and said, "That's my other son, John's house. He is also a carpenter." She paused for a moment and then said, "Wendy, your mother in-law, lives about two miles away."

I asked her, "Has everybody always lived in Brockway?"

"Yes, Roger went to the state of Colorada for two years. But, he came back."

It was hard for me to imagine that people spent all their lives in this tiny village where only two thousand people lived. What do people do for a living? What about entertainment? What keeps people in this village? I had too many questions brewing up in my mind. I wanted to meet other people in the family and in the village so I could talk to them and ask them about Brockway.

Gram and I got tired after talking and we both decided that it was time to go to bed. Holly had already gone to sleep by now. I crawled into the bed and laid next to her, thinking about my journey from Lucknow to Brockway.

Meeting Chub

~

I did not know who Rusty Wallace, Jeff Gordon, and Dale Earnhardt, Jr. were before I met my father-in-law. I also didn't know that Chub lived with him and that meeting that member of the family could almost give me a heart attack. After visiting Holly's dad for the first time and spending two hours—the longest two hours of my life—with him I left his place with the sound of an engine buzzing in my head, my heart pounding with fear, and my face cold and sweaty. I had never come so close to death.

On the occasion of Thanksgiving, I got the opportunity to meet my father-in-law for the first time. I was excited, but also nervous. Holly had mentioned to me several times that her dad was a strict parent and as a kid she was never allowed to do anything without asking his permission. Everything had a schedule in his household—bedtime, playtime, TV time, and study time—and anyone who broke the rules was made to stand in the corner. Once, in her early teens, Holly came home wearing a locket and told her parents it was given to her by a friend, Ashley. Her dad misunderstood the name and assumed it was a boy and scolded her for taking that gift. When she told him it was a girl he said, "It better be a girl," and told her she was not allowed to have a boyfriend before the age of thirty. She had also mentioned to me that he had a couple of Rottweiler dogs. That worried me because dogs and I don't get along too well. Somehow, they can tell by my body language that I am not comfortable around them and they decide to go after me.

Once, as a child, I was riding a bicycle on a street near my home in Lucknow. Since I wasn't tall enough to reach the ground sitting on the bicycle seat, I must not have been more than ten years old. I always had to look for a platform to get on and off the bike. I often asked my dad to hold the bicycle so I could get on—getting off was more of a challenge. That day, I remember, I saw an elevated platform in front of a house and decided to stop my bike there. But, I required some skill, since there was a group of dogs sitting two feet away from it. I had to do it without running over them. I don't remember exactly what happened, but as I approached, one of the dogs decided to go after me. Seeing the dog jump at me, I kept going instead of stopping. I saw it barking and racing behind me. My immediate reaction was to pedal harder and get out of its reach. As it came closer, it tried to grab my foot every time I brought it down to pedal. I decided to lift one foot up and pedal with the other. This slowed down my speed and the dog was clever enough to get around the bike and grab the other foot. I tried lifting both feet, but then I wasn't moving at all. In an effort to keep my foot attached to my leg and also race ahead, I lost my balance and fell down in an open drain by the side of the road. I hurt my knee and scratched my elbows and got my clothes soaked in the sewer water. By the time I got up, the dog had already left. I ended up causing more damage to myself by falling down than that little dog would have done.

When Holly told me about her dad's dogs, I did some research about Rottweilers. I found—on the internet—various explanations of their nature, strength, and characteristics, but one particular statement got stuck in my brain, "*...if your Rottweiler is around someone who is not capable of controlling it, you better have a loaded gun handy...*"

I grew up watching Indian films in which almost every romantic movie's plot was based on the hero struggling to convince his lover's father that he would be a good match. The heroine's dad is portrayed as a mean-looking, heartless human being. He doesn't care that his daughter is in love with this person and wants to marry him, but what he really does care about is whether he belongs to a family of equal status, education, or caste. He would go to any extreme to get rid of his daughter's lover. Since I had already married Holly without asking her dad, and she had broken all his rules—she started dating me several years ahead of his deadline of thirty, and even got married before that—I didn't know what to expect. I was terrified.

Holly told me that he lived twenty miles away from Brockway and it would take forty minutes to get there. We drove on narrow roads covered with compact snow that had wide open fields on both sides. Approaching from a distance, every now and then, I'd see a blue mailbox perched on a wooden stick by the side of the road, but no house in sight. After getting close, a house with a couple of pick-up trucks parked in front of it would appear sitting on top of a hill with a two hundred-foot-long driveway running all the way down to the mailbox. Some of the houses had horses in their front yard, barricaded by white wooden fences.

As we went along, some more randomly interspersed houses appeared along the way. A lot of them had their roofs covered with a sheet of snow, and their doors decorated with Christmas wreaths. I wondered about two things. First, why someone would choose to live in such a remote place? And second, why couldn't they be closer to each other instead of building their houses a mile apart, especially when there were so few of them? It seemed that I could count the number of houses on my two hands that I saw on the twenty-mile stretch.

After driving for more than three-quarters of an hour on the narrow roads, Holly made a sharp right turn and said, "We are close to Dad's house." I realized I had been looking out the window the whole time and she was busy driving and never asked me to help with directions. I asked, "Looks like you know the way." She said, "Of course, I grew up here." We drove for a few more minutes and then she turned the car on a snowy path marked by big tires. She said, "This is his driveway." At the beginning of the driveway was a sign—THIS PROPERTY IS GAURDED BY DOGS. We arrived in a huge open space where two old cars and a rundown SUV were parked. We parked our car and moved towards the door. The house was a two-story building and had a small porch in front. After knocking on the door we heard a voice saying, "WAIT A MINUTE, LET ME PUT THE DOGS AWAY!" It sounded like a large man's voice.

A few minutes later, a six-foot tall, bearded burly man opened the door. He was wearing a red checkered flannel shirt, a pair of blue jeans and a red hat that said "Miller Racing" in big letters. I gestured to shake his hand, but he grabbed my arm and pulled me towards him to give me a hug. The firm grip of his hands and powerful pull caught me unawares—I stumbled as he hugged me. He looked at me and said, "How ya doin' son?" Shaken by the handshake, I said, "I am fine, thanks!"

We sat down on a semi-circular couch that occupied half of the living room. A big flat-screen TV—that showed several cars running around in a circle—covered the wall in front of the couch, and family pictures were displayed on the other walls in the room. A skinny lady with a big grin came running out to give us a hug—Holly introduced her as Winnie, her stepmom. I said hello to her and returned a smile. Holly pointed at a young girl—she looked to be in her late teens—and said, "She is Hanna, my half-sister." I smiled at her and said, "Nice to meet you...I am Deepak." Hanna replied, "Of course…I know you are Deepak…got to see you finally." I was nervous and forgot that there was probably only one Deepak within the radius of a hundred—possibly more—miles in that area. I soon realized that the house was full of Holly's relatives—step-brother, step-sister, spouses and kids. They all came out, one after the other, into the living room to meet us. Ladies hugged me and gents shook my hand. I got the feeling that everyone was checking me out from the corner of their eyes, without making it obvious. It made me feel a little uncomfortable.

Coming to meet them for the first time, I wasn't sure what to say. My father in-law brought a bowl full of candies and put it in front of me on the glass-top coffee table and said, "Like candies?" I said, "Yes, I do." Encouraged by his friendliness I said, "You live pretty far away." He said, "Yeah…I like to live away from people." I looked at him and wondered why he wanted to live away from people. After a pause of a few seconds, he said, "I don't want no trouble and that's why I bought this house here…I don't like people living around me."

It didn't make sense to me. In India, when we moved houses, my father always made sure there were enough people in the vicinity and that's how we knew the area was safe. Also, a place without any people would have been boring and lifeless. Having lived all my life in apartments and in crowded places, I sometimes wished that my neighbors would leave us alone and not show up at our place without notice. Still, I would prefer a crowded place, with lots of people around, over a desolate area.

I told my father-in-law that I had never lived in such a remote place and that I always thought people in America lived in big cities like Chicago, Las Vegas, or New York. "Oh, I can't stand New York. I hate cities. One time, I accidently got on a highway that had a sign saying, 'New York 180 Miles'. I immediately got off the next exit," he responded, "I can't live in a city."

After a few minutes, he asked me to come to the dining room and offered me chips and filled a glass of water from a tap in the kitchen sink and said, "Try this water…it comes from ninety feet below ground." I hadn't asked for water but I took a swig from the glass. "Like it? It comes from ninety feet below ground," he said. I nodded, but I couldn't tell the difference between that water and the water that I had drunk in other places. He kept looking at me as if he wanted me to empty the glass. I did. He took the glass off my hands and filled it again and said, "Want more? It ain't no bottled water…it's fresh…comes from ninety feet below ground…I got my own well drilled in my backyard." I said, "No, thanks…I am not thirsty right now." He didn't know that tube wells are a common thing in India and almost every home in my village has one. He was proud to offer his ninety-feet-below-ground water to me. It was like my mother offering Holly bottled water and telling her it was no ordinary water from a tube well.

While I drank that special water, Holly played Boggle with the other people at the dining table. A few minutes later, my sister-in-law, Hanna, asked me, "Deepak, do you want to meet Chub?" Holly had mentioned the names of people in her family to me, but I didn't recall anyone called Chub. Curious, I said, "Who is Chub?" "Come on up, you'll find out," she said and started walking up the stairs. I followed and I saw her walking into a room. She gestured for me to come in. Since everybody else was downstairs, I wondered why I had to come to her room to meet Chub. Seeing my reluctance, she said, "Come in, Deepak…you gotta meet Chub." I walked in and saw her holding a four-foot long creature. Its textured green skin resembled a jackfruit and it had jagged spikes running across its spine; its sharp claws were bigger than my hand. Its long tail was wrapped around Hanna's neck. She said, "Hey Chub, do you want to say hi to Deepak?" and started giving it to me. Since I had never seen anything like that before, I thought it was a toy. As she brought it close to me, it snapped open its big jaws, revealing its saw-like teeth; a long forked tongue flashed out of its mouth and its big round bulging eyes popped open. Realizing that it was alive and real, my heart missed a beat. I ran out of the room and climbed down the whole set of stairs in two steps to get away.

My parents' home in India always had lizards—no bigger than three inches—running up and down the walls, but I had never touched or kept one as a pet; instead, I was always scared of them. Most people aren't bothered by their presence, but I am sure if one crawled up on my dead body, I would probably get up and start running. My mother once chased away a lizard that was sitting on my back while I was sleeping. She thought it was a good idea to do it without letting me know since I might have panicked.

The four-foot animal in Hanna's room almost gave me a heart attack. Panting, I came downstairs with a loud thud. At the bottom of the staircase, my sense of relief didn't last. The Rottweiler—he probably hadn't seen anybody jump like that—started barking. It was not an ordinary woof. With every spurt of barks he shook the wall hangings and other decorations in the room—my legs were shaking on their own. He snarled with fury in his eyes as he stared at me. He totally meant business. I tried calling my wife for help, but I couldn't speak because of the fear. After a couple of minutes when I got my tongue back, she finally heard me. She came running and asked, "What's the matter?" I meekly pointed at the dog. She laughed and said, "He won't hurt you, he is a very friendly dog." She turned around and let the dog loose and said, "Looks like Hanna scared you with her iguana?" While she grabbed him by the chain, he dragged her to get to me, keeping his eyes fixed—two inches below my chin—at my throat.

The kids continued running around the house and Holly resumed her game of Boggle as if nothing had happened. My heart was still racing and I felt helpless being around people who didn't understand how scared I was. Holly was the only person who could have helped, but she was busy playing and couldn't care less. The dog got quiet but he kept staring at me. I tried not to look at him and stood close to Holly's dad. I thought to myself that if I was destined to be attacked by a Rottweiler, I better be close to its owner. I asked him, "Can I have a glass of water, dad?" He filled the glass and gave it to me with a smile that said, "I told you...it's good water." This time I was really thirsty. As the dog walked by, brushing my legs, he said, "Watch out...he can knock your knees out if he walks through your legs...he doesn't know how heavy he is...the sucker is seventy pounds." Being in that house, with all those deadly animals on the loose, I tried to imagine what it would be like to be inside a cage with lions and the ringmaster in a circus. I have never experienced that, but I have a pretty good guess how it would feel.

The little five-year-old kids were running around the dog and making comments like, "Deepak, are you sure you don't want to play with Max?" I didn't say anything and stood at a safe distance. Holly's dad realized I was not being friendly with the dog. He said, "Deepak, come on, don't be a sissy, pet the dog." I still didn't do it. Soon, I became the butt of jokes throughout the household.

After a little while my father-in-law suggested I should see his collection of NASCAR memorabilia; he took me into his bedroom where he had a big bookshelf full of miniature versions of cars, tires, helmets and various hats worn by famous racers—he knew by heart who owned a particular hat and how many races he had won. There was another TV in his room that also was tuned in to a car race. While showing his collection of NASCAR items, he paused every two minutes and looked at the race on TV and expressed his frustration or exuberance. Before we got out of his room, he put a red hat on my head and said, "You can have it," and gave me a five-minute lecture about the driver whose picture was on the hat. I couldn't relate to his passion for the sport, but I appreciated his generosity.

After showing me his assortment of NASCAR items he said, "Put on your jacket…I wanna show you my garden." The back door opened into a huge backyard. We walked to one part of it where he had planted onions, peppers, tomatoes, squash, beans and cucumbers and many other vegetables a few months ago. I had always thought people in America were too busy working and didn't have time to cook and that they only ate frozen food. I never imagined that there could be people like my father-in-law who live hundreds of miles away from any city and grow their own vegetables. I enjoyed looking at his garden and it felt very nice to be outside and to talk about something different. He took me to the other part of his backyard and pointed out the wooden bird coop that he built himself. The coop—occupied by twenty-five chickens and ten turkeys—was big enough for both of us to walk through. He had heating lamps inside to keep the birds warm.

I asked him, "What do you do with these birds?"

He said, "Eat 'em!"

"They seem to be bigger than the ones I have seen in India."

"It's because I feed 'em well. The bigger they are the more meat you get. You see what I'm sayin.'"

When it was time to have dinner, he served me the food himself. It appeared to be some kind of half-cooked meat with no gravy or any spice. I nibbled on a small piece and realized it didn't have any taste. I asked him what kind of meat it was. Venison, I was told. He mentioned that it came from a deer that he had shot himself. I looked at him and he said, "Ain't it good? I cooked it myself." I said, "Yeah, it's good." I had never eaten deer before and especially one that had been shot by a bullet. Out of curiosity, I asked how long he had to chase the animal after he shot it. He smiled proudly and said, "It ain't goin' nowhere when I'm huntin'..."

Soon after dinner it was time to leave. Holly's dad packed us a big bag full of vegetables from his garden. Just when we got the car started and shut the door, my father-in-law came to me and rested his hands on the car window, lowered his head and said, "Deepak, can you do me a favor when you go to India next time?" I said, "Sure, what is it?"

"If I give you the name and address of this guy, could you go and punch him in his face?" Not sure what he meant, I looked at him with curiosity. "He keeps calling me to remind me to pay my credit card bills," he said and started laughing.

The Tour of Brockway

~

One day Papa decided to give us a tour of Brockway. After having lived in Charlottesville, Brockway seemed to be a completely different America. I didn't see a single man dressed in a suit and tie rushing to work with a briefcase in his hands or a woman wearing a furry coat, a pearl necklace, and carrying a classy purse. Most men wore flannel shirts, work overalls or jackets with NASCAR emblems. They drove American-made big pickup trucks or SUVs, not compact Hondas or Toyotas as they did in Charlottesville. Most of the vehicles were covered with some powder-like stuff and the snow on the roads was slushy and dirty, almost black in color. The cafes were called *Betsy's Coffee* or *Bill's Cafeteria*. The thing that struck me most was that every single person I saw in Brockway was white. I had never felt so out of place before; people turned their heads twice to look at me—especially kids, who walked backwards to watch me until I was out of their sight—like I was an animal in the zoo. Living in such a remote place, they may not have seen another person with a different color skin and hair.

About a decade ago when my English friend, Dan, expressed a desire to see country life in India, I took him to my village—my father's birth place. Some of the people there had never left their homes and with no electricity and no telephone connection, they had little exposure to the world outside their village. When the kids saw my friend—who is whiter than the whitest person I have ever seen—they thought he was some kind of monkey, with a pink face and yellow hair. I tried to explain that he was from a different country and people there are different, eat different food and speak a different language. They couldn't believe that there are some people who do not speak Hindi and *Dal*, lentil soup is not their staple diet. I had never imagined I would be in a similar situation one day—a brown person in a white land.

After driving around for a while, Papa stopped to run some errands on foot. Holly and I used that time to walk around 'downtown'—a quarter of a mile long stretch of a road which had parking on both sides; I noticed that the parking meter took only ten cents for an hour of parking. The whole downtown was made up of a few buildings—a bank, a thrift store, a hardware store, a pizza place, a post office, and a family run-cafeteria. We took a stroll up and down the street and we were done in less than ten minutes. We decided to go and have a cup of coffee at the only cafe in town. We went inside and I noticed that the place was mostly a gift store with little trinkets decorated on small shelves. There were two big thermoses on the top of the counter which were labeled, 'COFFEE'. The entire place was made of wood—the floor, shelves, walls, chairs—and the table top was a big oddly shaped wooden plank perched on a slightly tilted, round wooden log. As we walked around the store, a female voice shouted, "Holly!" My wife smiled and said, "Hi!" The lady responded, "I didn't know you were in town."

"Yes, we are visiting for a few days."

"Oh, okay…your brother was here a few days ago and I saw your mom yesterday."

It seemed like the owner knew my wife's family well. I asked my wife later, "How do you know her?"

"I went to school with her…she is the owner of the cafeteria."

After having a cup of coffee and a muffin we walked out of the place. Holly had to mail some letters so we stopped at the post office. The clerk behind the counter said, "Hey, Holly…I thought you were in India…the last time I saw Wendy she said you were still there."

"I got back a few months ago," she turned to me and said, "He is my husband, Deepak."

"Hi, nice to meet you…I went to school with Holly's mom."

I said, "Nice to meet you, Matt."

"Yeah…I finally get to see you in person…have heard so much about you."

After a friendly handshake we left the place. We walked down a few blocks and saw a white hand sticking out of a yellow school bus, waving frantically. I asked Holly, "What is she trying to do?" She turned to her right to look at the bus and said, "Oh my God, she is my mom's cousin, Bonnie."

Bonnie pulled the school bus beside us and stuck her head out, along with her already dangling hand, and screamed, "Hey Holly!!...Is that your husband?"

Holly said, "Yes he is...Deepak....Deepak she is Bonnie." Bonnie promised to come to our home and see us when she got off work.

Meeting people who knew Holly on the streets of Brockway made me feel as if it all had happened in my life before. My father moved to the city of Lucknow, when he was eighteen. When he finished his master's degree, he got a job in the city, and he could never go back to live in the village where he grew up, although he always wanted to return. He missed the place so much that he made sure he took our family to visit his parents and his brothers in the village at least twice a year. It took less than two hours on a bus to reach the last bus-worthy road from Lucknow. I remember arriving in the village, after riding a bullock cart on a dirt road for four miles; it used to be the longest part because our journey was interrupted by several relatives or acquaintances of my father. People would come up to us and my father would have to stop and chat with them. Meeting my wife's cousins and friends in Brockway felt the same way except I was in an American village and people were riding in SUVs and cars on snowy roads instead of bullock carts on a muddy path.

We got on the road again after bumping into some more friends and relatives of Holly. As we drove along, Gram pointed out homes of people she knew—she seemed to know everyone—and gave us a running commentary, "Deepak, this is where Dawkins live...he is a principal of a school...his son goes to school with Holly's cousin...and this is Benson's home...they have done a lot of work on their house this year...they go to the same church as us... and that is Sally's house...she went to school with Holly... she is married with two kids...and Deepak, look, that is my older sister Cathy's home," she turned to Papa and said, "Can we stop at Cathy's?" Without saying anything, Papa slowed down his car and turned the steering wheel to get off the road, crushing gravel and snow beneath his tires, and parked his car in front of an old looking house—Aunt Cathy's home. The house looked like an abandoned place with very little sign of life. The doormat was soaked in rainwater and it seemed no one had stepped on it for weeks. A lonely looking wooden rocking chair sat on the porch with clothes piled on it, and a pair of shoes filled with dirt laid next to the chair.

We walked in and saw that there were two beds in the living room along with a couch and a dining table. Aunt Cathy was sitting on a chair and I walked up to her to say hello; I extended my right hand to shake her hand, but instead of using her left hand she held my hand with her right hand and said, "This is my good hand." After shaking her right hand with my right hand, I sat down next to her. She smiled and said, "My left hand stopped working a long time ago." In the other corner of the room, a man was lying on the bed. I didn't notice him at first, but when I saw him I got up to say hello to him. He said in an alert tone, "Hi, I am Rob," and pulled himself up by holding on to the sideboards of the bed and sat up. He gave me a firm handshake with a grip that left my hand numb for a few minutes. I learned that Aunt Cathy and Uncle Rob were in their early eighties and lived alone in the house and Uncle Rob had had both legs amputated below the knee due to some disease. I noticed that he didn't have any teeth—his jaws and chin looked like a deflated balloon every time he said something—but it didn't stop him from talking. He told me that he was fond of two things: shopping at yard sales hunting and telling tall tales. When I asked him what kind of things he buys from a yard sale, he replied, "Anything and everything, but once I bought a used set of teeth for fifty cents and wanted to try them on, but mother didn't let me." He referred to his wife as mother. I also found out that he still goes to hunt even if that meant someone had to drive him and he had to be in his wheelchair. He had gotten special permission to shoot from inside his truck. While Uncle Rob was narrating his stories, I noticed Papa staring at the ceiling. I looked up, but didn't find anything remarkable about it. After a few minutes Gram said, "Papa, wake up!" Apparently, he had heard Uncle Rob's tales several times over the years.

After spending time at Uncle Rob and Aunt Cathy's, Gram, Papa, Holly, and I went to eat out. Papa drove us to one of his favorite places – some family restaurant.

The place looked like a barn from outside. A chubby old lady—who seemed to be in her late sixties or early seventies—with puffy white hair and dark red lipstick, greeted us at the door. She happened to be another relative of Holly's and we ended up talking to her for twenty minutes before she brought us the menu. Gram explained to me how the waitress—her name was Rinky—was related to her and Holly, but I don't remember now—I am sure I had forgotten it right away. But, what I cannot forget is that the lady had a very animated style of talking, with a knife in one hand and a fork in the other, she couldn't stop swinging her hands. She swiveled her waist and raised her eyebrows when she got excited, and she did it a lot. She sure was a happy woman. After forty minutes of talking to Rinky, and asking how each of her children and their children were doing and telling what Holly was up to recently and that she had spent some time in India and brought me back from there, we started ordering food. I ordered a chicken burger, Holly and Gram ordered some kind of dish with fish and Papa got steak. Pinky asked Papa if he wanted his steak to be well done, rare-medium or rare-rare. Papa said, "Pretty well done." When Pinky left us alone I asked Papa, "What is well done, rare-medium, and rare?"

He explained, "Well done is well cooked, rare-medium is not so well cooked and rare-rare is when you have to hold your meat down with a fork or it might take off."

Jazz and Beer

~

Soon after Holly and I arrived in Brockway for Christmas, Papa and Gram announced that we were invited to a party in their neighborhood. They told us it was a pot-luck dinner and everyone was supposed to bring some kind of dish with them; Gram had baked a rhubarb pie to take there. We got ready and jumped in Papa's van. After a few minutes of driving we pulled into a driveway that was mostly dirt and gravel. The headlights of Papa's van provided us with a view of the dark path and we arrived at an abandoned looking building. Gram mentioned that the party was organized in an old school building. I could hear children running and playing. When we walked inside I saw a long table stacked with food—meat balls, pasta, breads, cakes, pies—and another table had two big steel flasks and a tall pyramid of white Styrofoam cups, next to it. Another side of the big hall had about forty chairs that had fold-down desks attached to them. Toddlers, kids under ten, teenagers, young adults, middle-aged men and women and old people filled the place. One corner of the room had a big Christmas tree with a huge pile of presents under it.

Everyone seemed to know everyone except me. I needed to be introduced to people, but I realized that Papa, Gram and Holly got busy arranging stuff for the party and talking to people. I stood there for a few minutes, feeling a little lost. People looked at me and wondered who I was. I wanted to tell them that I was not trying to crash the party for free food and that I was a legitimate guest. A middle-aged woman came to me said, "Hi," in a tone that meant, "Can I help you?" Pointing my finger towards Gram and Papa, I said, "I am with her," trying to justify my presence at the party, "I came with Mr. and Mrs. Grant."

This particular condition of mine brought to mind an incident in India when a couple of my friends and I, at the peak of the marriage season when almost every street is jammed by marriage processions, decided to crash a wedding party and eat free food. Since we were not invited, we put on our best clothes, doused ourselves with cologne, buffed our shoes and blended into a wealthy-looking—girls in pearls and guys in ties dancing around an expensive car decorated with marigolds—marriage procession. It had to be a rich wedding; it wasn't worth taking the risk of getting publicly shamed and then thrown out of the party for ordinary food. We started dancing with the relatives and friends of the groom and made sure no one could tell the difference between us strangers and the groom's near and dear ones. A few minutes later the procession arrived at a swank-looking hotel and people started getting ready to be received by the bride's family. We walked through the heavily decorated entrance and quickly moved towards the food stall. There were at least five hundred people in the wedding. Although no one was checking, we wanted to come up with a good answer if someone asked us about our identity. One of us saw the wedding sign at the gate, "SANJAY WEDS RITA," and suggested we remember the groom's name. Every time someone looked at us suspiciously, we mentioned Sanjay's name and talked about him as if we had known him for years. Though a little scared, we enjoyed our time and the food at Sanjay's wedding. No one asked me who I was and we didn't have to give any explanation about our presence. At the party in Brockway, I found myself in a similar situation; although I was actually invited, I couldn't blend in as easily.

I noticed Holly talking to a group of girls who seemed to be her age, Gram discussing something with another set of women, and Papa talking to a group of men who seemed to be his age. I thought instead of standing in a corner, I should try to socialize. I walked towards Papa and he looked at me and said to his friends, "He is my grandson-in-law. He is from India." I smiled in acknowledgement. One of the guys from the group said, "You are an Indian but not the Woo Woo Woo kind, right?" Everyone started laughing. I smiled again without understanding the joke. Another person in the group said, "Jazzbeer...he was a great guy...he was from India too...he used to live in Brockway a long time ago."

Someone else said, "Yeah…Jazzbeer…he wore a turban and his kids did too." Another one got excited and said, "And his wife played Sitar." I heard someone else say from behind, "He had two cute little kids." I found myself surrounded by a group of people who were volunteering information about this person that I had never met and would probably never meet. It seemed as if they thought I really needed to know what Jasbir looked like, whether he wore a turban or not, whether his wife was a good sitar player or not. Also, their pronunciation of Jasbir made it sound like he drank a lot of beer and listened to Jazz music all the time.

People's memories of Jasbir made me remember an incident when I introduced my English friend, Dan, to my mother. I, now, feel sorry for him because he had to listen, for a long time, to my mother's description of this other English person—Bill—she had met some time ago. She told Dan every single detail of Bill's life, his family, his work, his looks, and how much she enjoyed talking to him. She didn't care to ask him if he was at all interested in hearing about Bill. Just like my mother tried to find a common thing to talk about, something that Dan could relate to and find interesting, people at the party in Brockway tried to make me comfortable by telling me about this one other Indian they had known. I am quite sure Jasbier and I are very different people, with different educational backgrounds, different religion, different language, different age group. I was later told that he came to work in Brockway in the early eighties. There was only one thing common between me and him—we were both Indians. Since I was the second

Indian Brockway folks had met in thirty years, it was a good enough reason for them to talk about Jasbir.

Soon, the party began. Someone announced that they were going to play a game. Every one sat down and they were given a card with nine squares drawn on it. We were asked to fill the squares with any number under thirty. One little girl was in charge of calling out random numbers. Anyone who had the number called by the girl could go to the tree and pick up a gift. The game started and the first number was called. Three people had that number and they picked up three gifts of their choice from below the tree. The next number was called and this time four people picked up gifts. The third number was called and then the fourth. All the gifts were gone by the time the sixth number was called. There were twenty four more numbers to be called and no gifts to be taken from the tree. People looked at each other with an expression that said, "Now what?" The moderator of the game looked at everybody and said, "Now the fun starts!" Nobody had the first clue about what she was talking about and how the game was going to be more interesting without any gifts.

"Alright, ladies and gentlemen, when the next number is announced, people are allowed to take anyone's gifts—anyone, I repeat, anyone—provided they have that number," the moderator said. At first people looked at each other with confusion. And a few seconds later they got a glitter in their eyes—when they understood the rule—their heads quickly revolved, screening everyone's possessions, as if to assess who had what.

"Got it?"

"Got it," everyone said in harmony.

It didn't matter that everyone in the hall was a stranger to me, and that I had never played this game before—I was just as excited as everybody else. The game started to grow on me. I was ready to take away people's gifts and couldn't wait for the next number to be called. The next hour was filled with people jumping over each other's gifts—taking it away and then losing it to the same person or someone different when the next number was announced and then waiting for an opportunity to get it back again. The place was filled with people screaming, "Oh no," "Oh Yeah," and "Oh, not again," "Watch out, I am gonna gitcha." After losing my gift several times, I managed to get it back finally. When the last number was announced, somehow, everyone ended up with at least one gift and they had to take turns opening them and showing what they got.

After a couple of hours of excitement, people started moving towards the food table. Holly introduced me to some of her high school friends who had married people from Brockway and settled down with two or three kids. After high school, they all had found jobs in and around their hometown and seemed content with life. Holly asked them about some of her other friends in town and if Mr. Krovosky—her favorite and a popular teacher—was still teaching in Brockway. She found out that after teaching in the Brockway Area High School for eighteen years he moved to a different town twenty miles away, in search of a better opportunity.

I nibbled on my food and stood around listening to them reminisce about their time. I didn't know anyone—Katy, Betsy, Bobbi, Duane, Joshua—they talked about and couldn't relate to anything they laughed over. We spent another hour talking and shaking hands with people. I enjoyed my time playing games, eating delicious home-cooked food, meeting Holly's friends, and learning about Jasbir. Finally when we got ready to leave, another gentleman came to me and said, "Jazzbeer used to have a girlfriend in Brockway...but he surprised all of us when he went to see his parents in India and came back with a wife."

Christmas with the In-Laws

~

In India I always looked forward to Christmas because that's when I got to eat delicious cakes; all the bakeries in the city of Lucknow would get busy with orders for XMAS. Some of my friends celebrated the festival and they invited me for the yummy feast. After tasting the dried-fruit cake at my friends' homes I always tried to find the same thing at different bakeries, but I never succeeded; I was told that they were a special order and they only baked them around Christmas time. I would have to wait for another twelve months for December 25th. But, to me, the festival was always limited to eating cakes—I never experienced celebrating Jesus' birthday.

After coming to America I got my chance to do so with my in-laws in Pennsylvania. The month of December arrived and Holly suggested we should start shopping for Christmas presents—a notion that I was unaware of. Christmas in India had nothing to do with gifts. People went to church, decorated their trees and gathered with friends and family to eat and celebrate, but I never saw people going crazy over buying gifts. In Charlottesville, the parking lots of all the shopping malls and major department stores became crowded in the month of December. Every other advertisment on the TV was about what people should buy for their near and dear ones and every other shop displayed their best Christmas deals.

Holly took me to the nearest Wal-Mart to shop for gifts. It was my first time at that store. I was happily surprised to see an Indian greeting me at the door. I had never imagined that a middle-aged Indian man's face could be so refreshing. The greeter looked at me with a conspicuous gleam in his eyes; I returned an equally warm smile. It was like meeting my brother after several years. I wanted to hug him and say, "Where have you been all this time? I missed you so much." After a warm handshake and a brief conversation about what part of India we came from and how long we have been living in the States, we moved ahead. I turned my head back at least three times to see if he was still looking at me. He sure was. As I moved ahead, I saw more Indians wearing light blue vests, some busily scanning people's purchases and some stacking the shelves and some just pushing carts filled with things like sanitary napkins, greeting cards, shoes, etc. I felt like I was back in India. I hadn't seen a single Indian in two months and all of a sudden there were so many of them. I heard a lot of Gujarati and Hindi being spoken around me; some of the workers had name tags such as, Shah, Patel, and Suthar.

Apart from the Indian workers, something else caught my attention in the store. I noticed people walking into the store empty-handed and leaving with carts full of stuff; some of them bought so much stuff that they required a couple employees from the store to help carry the purchases to their vehicles. Some other people just walked into the store and grabbed a computer, a TV, a camera or some expensive MP3 player and took it straight to the cashier to purchase it, without thinking twice. I had never seen people shop so mindlessly. It seemed like they had already decided to spend their money and all they had to do was to come and pick up the product. While I was browsing in the electronics section of the store, I heard a customer ask a salesman, "You got the latest portable DVD player?"

The sales person replied, "Yes, we do."

"How many you got?"

"Give me a sec," the salesman tapped some keys on his computer and said, "We have 9 in stock."

"Alright...give me seven of those...I am done shopping...everyone is getting the same thing this Christmas."

The customer walked out of the store with seven portable DVD players. It was amazing to see him spend more than fifteen hundred dollars in less than fifteen minutes. It seemed, to me, that the guy bought the Christmas presents because he felt obligated to give presents to his family, not because he wanted to.

I followed Holly in the store while she shopped for presents. She mostly bought small items—a can of Virginia peanuts, picture frames, greeting cards, etc. After that trip to the store, I started shopping at Wal-Mart more often; it provided me a change of scenery and I enjoyed talking to the Indian workers there.

A few days before Christmas we arrived in Brockway to celebrate the festival with my in-laws. Gram and Papa had a Santa Claus made of wood perched at the edge of their front yard. And, there were three Christmas trees in the house, one in the basement, and two in the living room, decorated with candy canes and several Santa Clauses. The kitchen counter was covered with Gram's cookie sheets which had colorful cookies on them. As I extended my hand to grab one of them, she slapped my wrist and quickly moved the tray away from me and then immediately brought it back with a cheeky smile on her face.

Gram and Papa started preparing for Christmas dinner for the next day—they were hosting it at their place and were expecting about seventeen people. I helped Papa carry tables and chairs from the basement to their dining room and set the dinner table. Two tables were joined to make room for everyone. Papa took out a red-colored table cloth and threw it at me, holding onto one end in his hands, and we pulled the cloth on to opposite ends of the table; he evened out the wrinkles with the palm of his hand and asked me to do the same. He then asked me to check that the cloth was hanging evenly on both sides of the table. Gram took out her good china to be laid on the perfect-looking dinner table. As she gingerly laid down the plates, cups and glasses, I asked her, "Gram, how long have you been using these dishes?" She straightened her back and smiled at me as if to say, "Are you ready for the whole story?" She said, "My father was a farmer and he grew onions and he grew big onions," she held her both hands a foot apart, "oh boy...some of them were this big...and he used to sell them to people...he taught me to grow onions, too...so when I learned to grow big ones like him, I sold them and bought these dishes."

I said, "Oh wow! When did you buy them?"

"You can say this is my onion money china," She laughed and said, "I bought 'em about fifty years ago."

Papa picked up a stack of plates and handed me half of them; he started laying them on the table, in front of each chair. When I started doing the same thing, he said, "Make sure you place them at the very edge of the table...there is a lot more that goes on this table." He, then, gave me a set of very Christmassy-looking paper napkins—green and red with several small Santas printed on them—and said to me, "Napkins snuggle right next to the plates."

I helped him lay all the dishes on the table and followed his instructions carefully. As I watched him do things around the house, I noticed that he followed a method in everything he did. He mostly wore a pair of blue faded jeans with a prominent crease running down the whole length of them, a red and white checkered flannel shirt and a pair of Velcro sneakers. If anybody asked him a question or said anything to him, he took a few seconds before he responded; he moved slowly, performed every action slowly, but perfectly—making his languid style look graceful. Rocking with his eyes closed on his recliner, he often seemed aloof to everyone around him, but he would say a name or an important number if people couldn't remember it in the middle of a conversation. Then Gram would say, "I thought you were sleeping."

"I'm listening," he would respond.

Around noon everyone gathered around the decked-out dinner table. After a short prayer by Papa, everyone started eating. After dinner Holly got up and brought a bunch of papers and started distributing them to everyone around the table. I didn't have any clue what that was about. I was handed a sheet of paper with a paragraph circled with a yellow highlighter. When Holly came back and sat next to me I asked her, "What am I supposed to with this?" She said, "These are the verses from the Bible and everyone has to read their assigned paragraph." I noticed some of the younger people at the table were complaining that they got a big part to read and some others were expressing their joy that they only had to read a couple of lines. My paragraph was about a hundred words and I had never read anything from the Bible; I felt like I was put under a spotlight. I was afraid that people may not understand when I read and may laugh at my accent. Everyone started reading their part and my heart started pounding heavily as my turn came closer. It felt like I was back in sixth grade again when the teacher asked every student in class to read a paragraph out of a chapter. It wasn't that I was bad at reading, but the fear that I would not be able to tell where the last person stopped reading—because I didn't pay attention and goofed around with my friends—when my turn came, almost killed me. A lot of times I read the wrong paragraph or the wrong page, causing a ripple of giggling in the classroom. The teacher would then ask me, "Deepak, were you sleeping?"

I definitely did not want that to happen on my first Christmas celebration with my wife's family. Although it was harder to understand everything said in a country accent, especially by people of different age groups, I paid very close attention to what everyone was reading and followed every word uttered. I got stiffer as my turn got closer and the fear that I may falter once again brought back the embarrassing memories of my childhood. Suddenly I felt something hit my knee under the dinner table and I ducked my head down to look. When I brought my head back up everyone started laughing. Of course, I had missed my turn once again and it was Holly's cousin who had tapped my knee to remind me. My face went pale with embarrassment and I think it was one of the most awkward moments of my life. Holly could tell that I was not comfortable. She grabbed my hand gently under the table and pointed at the paragraph where I was supposed to read. I read as fast as I could to hide my embarrassment.

After reading verses from the Bible, it was time for opening presents. Every one moved to another room where all the gifts were stacked under the ten-foot-tall Christmas tree. It was the youngest grandkid's duty to hand the wrapped-up colorful packages to everyone. Aaron stood up and started passing out the presents to people according to the names on the packages. The whole family took their positions—some sat on the floor, some on the couch and some of them just stood up. Everyone settled down with a pile of gifts in front of them. Now it was time to start opening the presents. I, somehow, had accumulated a fairly large heap of gifts, but Papa had the biggest mound in front of him, hiding his legs that hung from the rocking chair he was sitting on. He was the first to open a present. As he slowly removed the wrapper of the biggest box he had, everybody turned towards him and looked curiously. He removed the packing paper and cut open the box with a knife to find another box inside. Suspense filled the living room as he started opening it. He opened that box and saw that there was another box in it. Now people were really curious and I heard someone say, "Papa, you gotta have something good in there." He opened the last box and hoisted the present above his head and said, "This is from Gram." Everyone started laughing after seeing a box of cornflakes in his hand. Gram raised her voice in the room filled with giggles and laughter and said, "It was on sale...he already has everything he needs and I know he likes cornflakes." People laughed even harder. The next one in the circle opened his gift—it was a pair of socks—and said, "Oh...this is exactly what I needed...I have been meaning to buy some new socks for so long," He looked at the person who gave the socks to him, "Thank you so much." He seemed deeply thankful. When my turn came I opened a small envelope which said, "From:- Papa" It had a twenty-five dollar gift card for Wal-Mart. I thanked

Papa and he said, "I thought it would be an appropriate gift since you have been talking about going to Wal-Mart ever since you arrived here." I did mention a few times that I wanted to see what Wal-Mart in Brockway looked like and if there were any Indian workers there. (When I visited the Wal-Mart store near Brockway I did not see a single Indian employee; the only workers that I saw there had name tags such as Bobbi, Duane, Betsy and Bill.)

A couple of days after Christmas we went to church with Gram and Papa. We all rode in their van to the Presbyterian church which they had been attending for many years. Holly was going to sing in the choir with her mother and Gram. So, when we arrived at the church they went through a different door, and I followed Papa through the main entrance. Papa took the very last bench in the church, and I sat next to him.

The church had a very high ceiling with tall colorful windows on both sides. There were people of all ages— toddlers and people who looked to be in their nineties. Within a few minutes every single seat was occupied and the priest began his sermon. The choir sang hymns before and after the sermon with very high-pitched voices. Sitting next to Papa in the back row, I saw Holly dressed in a church robe and singing Christmas songs along with her family members, and it made me think that this was the 'Holly' her family and friends in Brockway had known for years. I could tell from the excitement in her eyes that she was happy to be back and singing and socializing with the people she grew up with. I noticed her mouth wide-opened and veins strained in her neck—she was trying to get the tone right and match the organ's sound in the background.

All the members of the choir were dressed in cream-colored robe and the priest was in a long black gown. Every now and then I heared the chants of "Praise the Lord!" and "Amen!" and "Hallelujah!"

After the service finished, a very old lady came up to me and held my hand and said, "Are you Deepak?"

"Yes, I am."

She spoke in an old-sounding voice, "Oh…you are so lucky…you got the smartest girl in town." She paused for a moment and looked at me with great attention and then said, "I am so glad to have met you."

I said, "Yes, it's nice to meet you too." As she walked away holding on to her stick, I felt someone put their hand on my shoulder, "Deepak!" I said, "Yes!"

"Oh my Gorsh…so nice to meet you," said another friendly old woman with big eyes, still keeping her hand on my shoulder. While she stood there, I felt someone grabbing my hand from behind. I turned around to see a third elderly woman. She said, "Are you Holly's husband?"

"Yes, I am Deepak!"

"You know, I have known Holly since she was a little girl…and I have known Wendy, her mom, since she was a little girl too…"

"I am sure."

"How long are you here for?

"Three or four days…"

"Oh…that is such a short time…but at least you could come."

"Yes, that's right," I said.

Soon, I was surrounded by several people whom I had never met, but all of them seemed to know me. I had never been in such a situation where everyone knew me; I hadn't done anything significant in my life to be this famous. Almost everyone in the church knew Holly and her family and since I was the only brown person there, it was easy for people to know who I was. I heard people whispering, "He is Holly's husband," and I overheard a group of elderly women who seemed to be in their eighties, saying things like, "Isn't he a handsome fella?" and "What a good looking man?" People kept coming at me from all directions, wanting to shake my hand and say hello. It was a strange feeling. People who had already shaken my hand and met me a few minutes ago were directing other people towards me, as if I were an important person.

More people came and shook my hand and congratulated me. We spent another hour talking to people in the church and shaking hands. I was overwhelmed with people's response to me. When we returned home, Papa wanted to take a picture of Holly and me to replace his granddaughter's old picture on his wall. He made us stand against a wall and clicked a picture and it went up on the wall—it felt surreal to see my brown face among several other white faces of my in-laws. Growing up in Lucknow, I had never imagined I would become a part of an American family in rural Pennsylvania.